FISHERMAN
RESOURCES

SOUL

SPIRITUAL COURAGE FOR THE BATTLES
OF LIFE

STRENGTH

PAM LAU

D0752587

SHAW BOOKS
an imprint of WATERBROOK PRESS

Soul Strength
A SHAW BOOK
PUBLISHED BY WATERBROOK PRESS
2375 Telstar Drive, Suite 160
Colorado Springs, Colorado 80920
A division of Random House, Inc.

All Scripture quotations, unless otherwise indicated, are taken from the *Holy Bible, New International Version*®. NIV®. Copyright © 1973, 1978, 1984 by International Bible Society. Used by permission of Zondervan Publishing House. All rights reserved. Scripture quotations marked (MSG) are taken from *The Message.* Copyright © by Eugene H. Peterson 1993, 1994, 1995. Used by permission of NavPress Publishing Group. Scripture quotations marked (NASB) are taken from the *New American Standard Bible*® (NASB). © Copyright The Lockman Foundation 1960, 1962, 1963, 1968, 1971, 1972, 1973, 1975, 1977, 1995. Used by permission. (www.Lockman.org.) Scripture quotations marked (NKJV) are taken from the *New King James Version.* Copyright © 1982 by Thomas Nelson, Inc. Used by permission. All rights reserved. Scripture quotations marked (NRSV) are taken from the *New Revised Standard Version of the Bible,* copyright © 1989 by the Division of Christian Education of the National Council of the Churches of Christ in the USA. Used by permission. All rights reserved.

ISBN 0-87788-091-3

Printed in the United States of America
2003—First Edition

10 9 8 7 6 5 4 3 2 1

To Brad—
my heart mate, mind mate, soul mate

CONTENTS

ACKNOWLEDGMENTS

I am deeply grateful to Laura Barker and my editor, Elisa Stanford, who believed in doing a new thing by taking on this project. Elisa guided and mentored me through this venture with skill and patience, and Jennifer Lonas oversaw the rest of the editorial process with diligence and sensitivity. You are all a joy to work with!

I'd first like to thank the Women's Bible Fellowship at Newberg Friends Church where I first taught this journey to soul strength. A special thanks to Melva Brandt, Lisa Church, and LaNeal Miller for their timely and much-needed words of encouragement.

To those whose noble friendship I cherish because, as Robert Burns says, you "dare to be honest and fear no labor"—I thank you for your grand gift of godly and wise counsel. These same people read parts of this study and offered contributions and suggestions: Daralice Boles, Kathleen Kambic, Bradley A. Lau, James Lincoln, and Joan Tompkins.

For the four people who continue to parent me, Thomas Havey, Sandra Havey, Jerry Lau and Le Anne Lau—God consistently speaks to me through you. I also want to acknowledge our close friends Mark and Miriam Hall and Neal and Susan Ninteman. Our covenant relationship in seeking soul strength as families has encouraged our family deeply.

Finally, I say "thank you" to the Master of my soul, the Lord Jesus Christ, for whom this book is ultimately written.

INTRODUCTION

In his book *The Prince*, Niccolò Machiavelli wrote, "It is unnecessary for a prince to have [honor, integrity, and character], but it is very necessary to appear to have them."[1] He concluded that the only way to succeed in life is to pretend.

Pretending to have strength does seem like a good solution at times when we're feeling weak. But if we're looking for a more authentic relationship with God, we know that *pretending* to be strong in him just doesn't work. It only leaves us feeling empty—wanting more, but settling for less. God never expects us to pretend to have spiritual strength, nor does he want us to just get by in life with our weakness of character. Rather, he wants us to receive and use with precision the specific pieces of armor he has given us.

I don't have the formula for being strong, but I know that God has been teaching me about my own weaknesses (even in the midst of writing this study) so that I might experience his strength. I testify with my heart and mind that I know the difference between living in my own strength and living by God's: It is what I call soul strength! The journey to soul strength is one I live every day.

Developing the skills for dressing your soul in God's strength is an inward journey that transforms your character. I've learned more in this process than I can ever write about, but I want to highlight three principles in particular that will help us define soul strength.

First, soul strength is a journey that requires us to be mobile. In this study I will often say that we are moving. We have a destination, and that

---

1. Niccolò Machiavelli, "Concerning the Way in Which Princes Should Keep Faith," chap 18 in *The Prince* (Chicago: University of Chicago Press, 1988.)

destination is God—and his will for us. In order to receive God's instruction on how to use his armor, we must walk, run, or crawl *toward* him!

Second, soul strength requires that we learn to use the skills our Maker designed. These skills are taught only in heaven's classrooms. I would like to guide you through the soul-strengthening skills God has taught me, but only so that you can listen, practice, and experience these skills for yourself. (When I need motivation to exercise more, I read articles or books on working out, but it doesn't do me any good if I don't get my running shoes on and hit the pavement!)

Finally, we need to look at *why* we need soul strength. A spiritual power struggle is going on in this world! The Enemy is *real,* and he "prowls around like a roaring lion looking for someone to devour" (1 Peter 5:8). But let's not ascribe too much power to him; the Creator and Lover of our souls is much greater, and he enables us to be strong smack in the middle of this spiritual battle.

The Bible uses the word *soul* to mean "self, someone, a person, life." Our soul is the part of us that is eternal. Do you need strength in your whole self, your eternal self? Are you in a place where you really want to know how to use God's armor? Since God hand-knitted our souls together—not even science and technology can do this!—we need to discover the weapons and tools he intends for us to use.

STRENGTH FOR THE BATTLE

For a tiny group of people in Ephesus at the time of the early Christian church, *pretending* to be strong was not an option. They had just renounced a party lifestyle and satanic worship to follow the Lord Jesus Christ. Now that they had been delivered from the powers of darkness and a false perception of strength, they had to face their true selves: They were weak, helpless, and poor in spirit. Their only hope for true strength was to cling to Jesus.

The apostle Paul knew that their former lifestyle offered no strength at all but was a futile cover-up for sin, fear, pretense, and insecurity. To escape a life of despair and emptiness, these new Christ-followers had to keep moving toward God. In his letter to the church in Ephesus, Paul instructed the believers to "be strong in the Lord" (Ephesians 6:10), implying that they would not last long if they tried to live in their own strength. He used the image of armor so the Ephesian Christians—as well as those who followed—could visualize the spiritual protection God had given them.

So what does this spiritual protection look like? And how do we know we're moving in the right direction—toward God? Given the variety of "spiritual" movements available to us today, it's no wonder so many confused souls try on the flimsy designer wardrobes of faith instead of the solid armor of God.

Eleven hundred and eighty years before Paul wrote about the armor of God, Joshua and the Israelites were asked to *literally* move from a place of emptiness and defeat to a place of strength and freedom. Like the Ephesians, Joshua and the Israelites had to cut themselves away from their old way of living. The Israelites had to sever themselves from forty years of deeply rooted habits and receive God's strength and courage to win the battles before them. Likewise, Paul reminded the Ephesians that they were in a constant battle with the forces of darkness. Herein lies a splendid similarity between the book of Joshua and the description of the armor of God in Ephesians: Whatever we need to fight and win the battle is already available to us. We do not have to be empty, fearful, insecure, or weak in character; strength is ours for the receiving! Paul put it ironically: "When [we are] weak, then [we are] strong" (2 Corinthians 12:10).

I can tell you from my own spiritual journey that being clothed in soul strength is not a simple, one-time decision—no matter how strong and passionate I feel! Figuring out the difference between my will and the Christ-character in me creates spiritual friction throughout my day.

Perhaps that's what Paul meant when he said that he struggled with the energy of Christ (see Colossians 1:29). This is so true! I struggle with my faith constantly. For me to deny this struggle would be fake, inhuman. Because life is cyclical, the struggle is so intense at times that it seems unbearable. So I struggle. Good, bad. Christ, me. Envy, grace. Disbelief, acceptance. Resentment, repentance. Round and round I go. This moment-to-moment inner struggle is as natural as breathing—it's ongoing, repetitious, rhythmic, necessary, sometimes shallow, other times full and deep. Yet God continues to strengthen me in the process. That's freeing news!

BEFORE YOU BEGIN

The purpose of this study is to guide you to a place where you can hear the voice of the One True God instructing you *how* to put on his full armor during the intense battles you are facing right now or may face in the future. You can do this study alone, with a companion, or with a small group of people I like to call a Soul Group, a cross between a book club and a Bible study.

As you read, you will be introduced to eight soul-strengthening skills. Within each lesson, you will find an introductory question designed to get you thinking about the main topic. Then you will move into three different approaches to studying a specific truth about soul strength:

1. *Inductive Bible study*—In the sections called First Looks, you will be asked to think about and discuss the passage you have read, write out verses in your own words, look at the original language of the text, and learn about the background of the text. (In your reading, you will come across literary terms such as *character, setting, antagonist,* and *climax* that are explained in the context of the question or text.)

2. *Creative exercise study*—In the Taking It In sections, you will write out your thoughts and sometimes be encouraged to act on what

you discover. These exercises are designed to help you put on God's armor and are especially useful in a group setting.

3. *Literary study*—Making It Real sections will guide you through a variety of literary selections from people such as C. S. Lewis, Jonathan Edwards, Anne Bradstreet, and Shakespeare that build upon other parts of the lesson. After each literary piece I've included some probing questions to help you make the connection between these stories, the theme of the lesson, and your life.

You will be reading a passage from Scripture, thinking through some of the facts related to the passage, and then doing a creative exercise to see how the truth of that passage relates to your life. Then you will parallel that truth again with an excerpt from a piece of literature.

I hope you *enjoy* reading the biblical accounts as well as the stories and literary works presented in this study. They are part of God's invitation to us to receive his soul strength. At the back of the book, you will find leader's notes to help you think through some of the questions more thoroughly, whether you are leading a group through the guide or going through the guide on your own. Questions that have leader's notes are marked with a ✔ in the text.

Soul Strength is designed to help you wrap your mind, heart, and soul around the truth of God's Word. It is not meant to be like a daily devotional that makes you feel guilty if you don't have time to do it. It is intended as a guide you can pick up whenever you need soul strength, a guide that reflects the cyclical nature of our spiritual journeys as we move closer to God. I would suggest starting with the first study, but then feel free to pick up the guide and turn to whatever study addresses the piece of God's armor you particularly need at the moment. When you need the helmet of hope, for instance, read study 7. When you need the shoes of peace, turn to study 5.

Before you begin, think about these three questions:

1. On what do you stand firm when your heart is melting?

2. How do you move toward God when your mind is struggling?

3. What does it mean to you to believe something with both your head and your heart?

Clothing our souls in strength means to literally *wear* the Lord Jesus Christ (see Romans 13:14). As we live our twenty-first-century lives, we can hear the whispers of Jehovah, "Be strong and courageous." He said this to Joshua three times in the first nine verses of the first chapter of Joshua. In the original language these words mean "to bind tight," "to twist or roll together," "to fasten upon," "to be sure." When Joshua heard these words, and when the Ephesian Christians read Paul's letter, they did not stand up and resolve to pursue a more self-sufficient lifestyle. They resolved to move toward God, to bind with or twist together with or fasten upon God himself. And because they made that choice to receive God's strength, they endured.

My friend, the God of Israel gives strength and power to his people. His voice alone is powerful. Psalm 29 creates an image of God's voice breaking and splintering large cedar trees and those same trees skipping like calves (see verses 5-6, NKJV). I believe a new time has arrived as this generation of believers stands on the banks of the Jordan River ready to move, desiring strength, wanting to stand firm on a faith that's real. Do you sense a stirring in your spirit? Let's prepare to be clothed in soul strength.

ONE

PREPARING FOR BATTLE

Standing Firm, Standing Still

JOSHUA 1; EPHESIANS 6:10-11;
ROMANS 8:5-11

Finally, be strong in the Lord and in his mighty power.

—EPHESIANS 6:10

When I looked up the word *strong* in the *Oxford Universal Dictionary,* I found twenty-three definitions. The first was "physically powerful." Another read, "the capacity for taking much drink without becoming intoxicated." Immediately following, however, was a definition that captured my attention: "Having great moral power for endurance or effort; firm in will or purpose; brave, resolute, steadfast." One definition actually used the word *hale,* which is a root word for *holy.* God wants us to be holy as he is holy—separated in attitude from our culture, *strong* in character.

BREAKING GROUND

How would you define *strong*? What image or object do you think of when you think of something that has strength?

PAUSE FOR INSTRUCTION

In Ephesians 6, the apostle Paul wrote, "Be strong in the Lord and in his mighty power. Put on the full armor of God so that you can take your stand against the devil's schemes" (verses 10-11). *The Message* puts it this way: "God is strong, and he wants you strong. So take everything the Master has set out for you, well-made weapons of the best materials. And put them to use so you will be able to stand up to everything the Devil throws your way."

The definition of *stand* is "to take an upright position," "to endure." It also indicates a pause or delay. In this chapter we will look at the three-point connection between being strong, putting on God's armor, and taking our stand. We will also look at how putting on the full armor of God and standing firm are parallel actions that work together. We stand firm—or pause—in order to put on God's armor, and we put on God's armor to stand firm. Together these actions give us strength in the Lord.

When I am experiencing weakness, despair, or anger, the last thing I want to think about is enduring with effort and putting on some imaginary pieces of battle gear! During those times my weaknesses are clear—I cannot find strength within myself to cope with life's demands. But giving in to weakness sends the Enemy a white flag. It's in those moments that Paul's advice doesn't seem so way out after all. The unseen powers of darkness are at war, and if I'm not prepared for the battles, I will live defeated and will struggle to stand firm. I need to *pause* to put on God's armor and then stand firm as I wait to receive God's battle instructions.

Read Joshua 1.

First Looks

� 1. Who are the main characters in this passage?

⚤ 2. What is the setting? What did God promise to give the Israelites?

3. How did Joshua communicate God's instructions to the people? What was the Israelites' response to Joshua's instructions?

⚤ *Indicates further information in Leader's Notes*

4. Write one sentence that summarizes this passage.

Read Ephesians 6:10-11.

5. Rewrite this passage in your own words.

6. According to verse 10, what's our first instruction?

THE CALL TO PREPARE

Take note that God told the Israelites—this mass of 2.5 million people—to "get ready" to cross the Jordan River (Joshua 1:2). In Ephesians 6:11, Paul's phrase "put on" parallels God's instructions to Joshua and the Israelites to "get ready." Paul admonishes us to put on the full armor of God "so that [we] can take [our] stand" and get ready for when God moves us.

But we see another parallel between Ephesians 6 and Joshua 1: There's a struggle, a fight, some kind of event to prepare for. To stand firm as we prepare for this battle, we must follow three directives:

1. Prepare carefully. Raising three girls under the age of six can plunge me into moments of sheer chaos. What gets me in trouble most of the time is my lack of preparation. No matter how I arrive at our destination—carefully dressed, on time, in good spirits—if I do not bring food, drinks, books, my cell phone, or my checkbook, I will not accomplish what I set out to do. And I will pay the price for not being ready, because getting three girls out of the house on time is no easy task! I'm really my own worst enemy if I don't take the time to think about what I will need when I reach my destination. That's how we should think about the armor of God. He knows what spiritual battles we are about to face, and he has what we need to prepare ourselves.

2. *Put on the full armor.* What is the full armor of God? The original language uses the word *panoplia. Pan* means "all" and *hopla* means "arms or weapons." As you take a closer look at the separate pieces of the armor in the lessons that follow, think about the fact that each day you pause and consider what clothes to wear. For example, before I get dressed for the day, I've already changed twice: once from my pajamas to my workout clothes, and once from my workout clothes to my daytime clothes. When late afternoon rolls around, I'm ready to put on another outfit that doesn't feel so worn from the day's work. The analogy is simple, I realize, but most of us in modern America would not live our daily lives without fully dressing ourselves in clothes that are appropriate for each occasion. I think that's Paul's point here: God has a closetful of spiritual clothes for us to wear, and dressing ourselves in the complete outfit provides the best defense against the day's battles.

3. *Pause for instruction.* Before we can put on God's armor, we must pause to listen for his instructions. God told Joshua to "stand firm" and "be strong and courageous." These are the same words Paul used when he wrote his letter to the Ephesians. Note that the words "be strong" were *spoken* aloud; the Israelites actually paused to *hear* the words with their ears. Through Joshua they heard God's instructions to "be careful to obey all the law." Paul's words to the first-century Christians—"be strong in the Lord" and "put on the full armor of God"—were *written down* for them to *read.* Like the Israelites, these believers had to pause to listen to God's instructions. So, too, we must pause to read the words God is speaking to us. After the Israelites had heard God's instructions, they physically moved one foot in front of the other to cross the Jordan River. Like the Ephesians,

Christians today pause to hear or read God's words of instruction and then move their *wills* and their *minds* in obedience to him. We can move because we have first stood still to hear God's instructions. Our souls stand firm when we wait for clear direction, when we wait to see what spiritual battle God wants us to fight.

Taking It In

7. How would you describe the tone of Paul's words? the emotional impact (see Ephesians 6:10-11)?

8. God told Joshua to "be strong and courageous" three times in Joshua 1. How would you describe someone who is not being strong? How would you describe yourself when you're not strong?

9. God promised not to leave Joshua. He actually said, "I will be with you; I will never leave you nor forsake you" (Joshua 1:5). What do these two statements—"Be strong" and "I will never leave you"—suggest about how God relates to people?

10. The phrase "Be strong *in* the Lord" (Ephesians 6:10, emphasis added) may seem a bit nebulous. What do you think it means?

11. Reread Joshua 1:7-8. What did God give the people? What were they expected to do with it? What would you say dominates your inner life more: Scripture or your own thoughts or something else?

12. With Bible in hand, stand up (find a nice view) and read aloud the first chapter of Joshua, replacing the name "Joshua" with your own name. Put your whole self into this exercise, including your imagination! Walk around your yard, your home, your office, or wherever you are, and imagine Joshua's receiving God's advice to be strong and courageous. Transfer that message to your own spirit.

13. List below some of your own weaknesses and then humbly ask God to be your strength and courage in each weakness.

LISTEN AND ACT

Joshua and the Israelites were about to receive and enter a land flowing with milk and honey. In other words, it was an incredible place to put down some roots and raise a family. But to keep the land, the people would have to obey God's Law.

Years earlier God told Moses how the people of Israel should live, and Moses wrote these commandments in the first five books of the Old Testament. Jewish rabbis call these books the Pentateuch. The Pentateuch is considered a literary masterpiece as well as a tremendous revelation of God. (It's remarkable that the history, the moral standards, and the government records of so small a nation have been so fully preserved. The stories alone are fascinating.)

The 2.5 million Jewish people described in the book of Joshua stood in the exact same spot their parents had stood forty years earlier, the center stage of a battle between good and evil. (Numbers 13 and 14 detail the earlier story.) They faced the same choice their parents did: to obey God or hold back.

Their parents held back. When Moses' spies returned from the first scouting of the Promised Land, they had one report but two contradictory perspectives: Ten of the twelve spies expressed fear of the giant people they saw; they said it was "a land that devours its inhabitants" (Numbers 13:32, NASB). Two of the spies, Joshua and Caleb, judged the situation differently and reminded the people that the God who had parted the Red Sea would be there to fight for them. The people then faced a spiritual struggle, a struggle they lost because they thought only of their own strength and saw that it wouldn't stand up to the challenge before them.

The root of the word *obedience* means "to listen and act." I believe the Jewish people were listening. They struggled spiritually, though, because they stopped valuing God's Word, and their actions reflected their values. They feared what they saw and dismissed what they couldn't see. They gave in to bitterness, disbelief, cynicism, and anger. That generation did not inherit the ripened fruits of goodness, trust, and God-reliant faith.

We lose spiritual battles when we do not listen and act in response to God's Word. Our attitudes, habits, and actions become a spiritual battleground when *the Word of the Lord departs from our mouths* (see Joshua 1:8). In Joshua 1, we read that the Israelites both heard and acted on what God told them, so they were ready to enter the Promised Land.

Today, we also are called to act on the Word of God. The armor of God gives us the ability to conquer the Enemy with the eternal weapons of faith, truth, peace, righteousness, hope, Scripture, and prayer. It is a symbol of God's all-sufficiency. When we read and act on the Word of God, we are putting on his armor and preparing to fight victoriously in spiritual battle. Knowing Scripture allows us to stand firm in the active strength of the Lord.

"Be strong in the Lord." When you are angry, listen to God whisper these words to you. When you feel too weak for God to use, remember that God spoke these words to a man who knew he was useless without the strength of the Lord. When you are in despair, replay the scene in Joshua 1 in your mind. When you feel lonely, stand still and remind yourself of God's very real presence. When you are tired or sick, let those words remind you of the One who is your strength. When your mind insists on knowing only the facts, move away from your disbelief and believe in the spiritual realm. We cannot do this life alone. No matter who we are by family birth or social and financial status, and no matter how much education and intelligence we may have been given—yes, the world applauds the best and brightest—remember that God gives power to the faint, and he perfects his strength in weakness.

MAKING IT REAL

C. S. Lewis's *The Screwtape Letters* gives us a peek at how the invisible spiritual battle plays out in our daily lives. In this book, the evil Screwtape, a

"chief" devil in Satan's service, is giving instructions to his nephew, Wormwood, on how to keep one person from going over to the Enemy's (God's)
side.

Read Romans 8:5-11 and the following excerpt.

THE SCREWTAPE LETTERS BY C. S. LEWIS[1]

My dear Wormwood,

I note what you say about guiding your patient's reading and taking care that
he sees a good deal of his materialist friend. But are you not being a trifle
naïf? It sounds as if you supposed that *argument* was the way to keep him out
of the Enemy's clutches. That might have been so if he had lived a few centuries earlier. At that time the humans still knew pretty well when a thing was
proved and when it was not; and if it was proved they really believed it. They
still connected thinking with doing and were prepared to alter their way of
life as the result of a chain of reasoning. But what with the weekly press and
other such weapons we have largely altered that. Your man has been accus-
tomed, ever since he was a boy, to have a dozen incompatible philosophies
dancing about together inside his head. He doesn't think of doctrines as pri-
marily "true" or "false", but as "academic" or "practical", "outworn" or "con-
temporary", "conventional" or "ruthless". Jargon, not argument, is your best
ally in keeping him from the Church. Don't waste time trying to make him
think that materialism is *true!* Make him think it is strong, or stark, or courageous—that it is the philosophy of the future. That's the sort of thing he cares
about.

The trouble about argument is that it moves the whole struggle onto the
Enemy's own ground. He can argue too; whereas in really practical propa-
ganda of the kind I am suggesting He has been shown for centuries to be

---

1. C. S. Lewis, *The Screwtape Letters* (Uhrichsville, Ohio: Barbour, 1990), 11-4. Used by permission.
Copyright © C. S. Lewis Pte. Ltd. 1942.

greatly the inferior of Our Father Below. By the very act of arguing, you awake the patient's reason; and once it is awake, who can foresee the result? Even if a particular train of thought can be twisted so as to end in our favour, you will find that you have been strengthening in your patient the fatal habit of attending to universal issues and withdrawing his attention from the stream of immediate sense experiences. Your business is to fix his attention on the stream. Teach him to call it "real life" and don't let him ask what he means by "real".

Remember, he is not, like you, a pure spirit. Never having been a human (Oh that abominable advantage of the Enemy's!) you don't realise how enslaved they are to the pressure of the ordinary. I once had a patient, a sound atheist, who used to read in the British Museum. One day, as he sat reading, I saw a train of thought in his mind beginning to go the wrong way. The Enemy, of course, was at his elbow in a moment. Before I knew where I was I saw my twenty years' work beginning to totter. If I had lost my head and begun to attempt a defence by argument I should have been undone. But I was not such a fool. I struck instantly at the part of the man which I had best under my control and suggested that it was just about time he had some lunch. The Enemy presumably made the counter-suggestion (you know how one can never *quite* overhear what He says to them?) that this was more important than lunch. At least I think that must have been His line for when I said "Quite. In fact much *too* important to tackle at the end of a morning", the patient brightened up considerably; and by the time I had added "Much better come back after lunch and go into it with a fresh mind", he was already half way to the door. Once he was in the street the battle was won. I showed him a newsboy shouting the midday paper, and a No. 73 bus going past, and before he reached the bottom of the steps I had got into him an unalterable conviction that, whatever odd ideas might come into a man's head when he was shut up alone with his books, a healthy dose of "real life" (by which he meant the bus and the newsboy) was enough to show him that all "that sort of thing" just couldn't be true. He knew he'd had a narrow escape and in later years was fond of talking about "that inarticulate sense for actuality which is our ultimate safeguard against the aberrations of mere logic". He is now safe in Our Father's house.

You begin to see the point? Thanks to processes which we set at work in them centuries ago, they find it all but impossible to believe in the unfamiliar while the familiar is before their eyes. Keep pressing home on him the *ordinariness* of things. Above all, do not attempt to use science (I mean, the real sciences) as a defence against Christianity. They will positively encourage him to think about realities he can't touch and see. There have been sad cases among the modern physicists. If he must dabble in science, keep him on economics and sociology; don't let him get away from that invaluable "real life". But the best of all is to let him read no science but to give him a grand general idea that he knows it all and that everything he happens to have picked up in casual talk and reading is "the results of modern investigation". Do remember you are there to fuddle him. From the way some of you young fiends talk, anyone would suppose it was our job to *teach!*

Your affectionate uncle

SCREWTAPE

14. Consider the following quotes from *The Screwtape Letters*:

> I had got into him an unalterable conviction that, whatever odd ideas might come into a man's head when he was shut up alone with his books, a healthy dose of "real life" (by which he meant the bus and the newsboy) was enough to show him that all "that sort of thing" just couldn't be true.

> Much better come back after lunch and go into it with a fresh mind.

Does a healthy dose of "real life" have the same effect on you? Explain.

What tactics does the Enemy use in your life to distract you from what is "real" or true (important)?

15. Satan often taunts us with thoughts that penetrate our souls with fear and cripple us emotionally. With what kind of thoughts does Satan taunt you? What encouragement does Romans 8:6 give you?

16. What have you learned from this study that will help you fight this spiritual battle?

TWO

A FOREVER RELATIONSHIP

Trusting in the Character of the King

JOSHUA 1; EPHESIANS 6:10-17

Fuss and feverishness, anxiety, intensity, intolerance, instability, pessimism and wobble, and every kind of hurry and worry—these, even on the highest levels, are signs of the self-made and self-acting soul.

—EVELYN UNDERHILL, *The Spiritual Life*

During the nine months of our engagement, Brad and I lived about six hours apart in different states. We took turns traveling to see each other, usually on weekends, and at the end of each weekend together, we found it difficult to part. Mondays were a constant battle for me, particularly because I worked in a large advertising office where my women coworkers continually reminded me that I was throwing away my career to get married. Most comments I could let slide, but every so often someone's comment about how Brad would change after we married would get my thoughts moving in a negative direction. I could hardly wait until our next weekend together so I could figure out who this man really was!

It was during those weekend visits that I began to recognize an amazing characteristic in the man I was about to marry: He had a tender heart embedded in a rock-solid spirit. I saw this tenderness in the things Brad did for me in the present and in the things he did for us for the future. I was eager to know more about this man with such a strong character. Whenever I doubted that Brad was marrying me for noble reasons, I spiraled into insecurity. Whenever I focused on his character, I was free to trust in his genuine commitment to a forever relationship with me.

I find parallels here with our relationship with God. The Joshua story is about the Israelites' recognizing their Lover's voice and enjoying intimacy—a place of rest—because they were secure in their relationship with him. The Lord God of Israel provided the people of Israel with opportunities to know him through words, a godly leader, and miraculous circumstances. (If Israel's spiritual growth had been rated at this place and time, they would have received a ten; in this brief moment of history, they got it!) God wrote the Book of the Law to make his ways known, and it seems that God's character, God's voice, and God's plans were well known and accepted by the people at this time. The intimacy that had been established with God resulted in a people whose attitudes were free of "fuss and feverishness, anxiety…and worry."

Relating well to God gives us freedom, rest, and strength. The Enemy will use our own thoughts and the comments of others to keep us from "possessing" a deep and intimate relationship with God. But standing firm and putting on the full armor of God is easier when we contemplate and trust in the character of our King.

BREAKING GROUND

When you are under pressure because of sudden changes, deadlines, a sick child, a move, or just the details of life, what is your response to God? Do you tend to cling to him or resist him? Explain.

READY TO GO

The Israelites in Joshua 1 had it relatively easy when it came time to get ready to move from one place to another; they knew exactly how to prepare because they had been moving around for thirty-eight years. With bags already labeled and the family lined up, the Israelites were ready to go at a moment's notice. Not a hint of hurry or worry is found in the beginning of the Joshua story.

Read Joshua 1 again.

FIRST LOOKS

1. Who initiated the Israelites' move across the Jordan River to the land of Canaan?

2. What was God's first instruction to Joshua (verse 2)?

3. Exactly how did God command Joshua to respond to this move (verse 6)?

4. List the promises God made to Joshua in verses 1-9.

5. For what did Joshua need to be strong? (Read verse 7 carefully.)

Read Ephesians 6:10-11 again.

6. What do you learn about the character of God from these verses?

COME TO REST

My husband spends hours preparing to watch the Denver Broncos play football. He clears his schedule, invites a friend over, stocks up on snacks, and puts on his obnoxious blue and orange sweatpants. I want to be in the room just to feel and appreciate his unbridled enthusiasm as he makes every effort to prepare for the game! In the book of Joshua, the Israelites were preparing for their own big event. The mood and tone were electric because they knew God was in charge of this move. When people prepare for and share in a big celebration together, it almost always reflects a deep level of intimacy and commitment. The feeling is contagious.

The beginning of the Joshua story has relationship and intimacy written all over it. Everybody was happy and getting along. God said, "Be strong," Joshua immediately responded, and the people of Israel eagerly expressed support! Do you sense the excitement? Keep in mind that these people were headed for battle, but because of their deep relationship with God, the battle was not their focus; God's promises to them were!

The plans were straightforward, almost like wedding plans or details for a large celebration:

1. Be careful to follow the guidelines.
2. Be strong and courageous.
3. Tell everybody the good news.
4. Even if you're not making the trip, we could use your help in the move.

Commentators often note that the Israelites' "possession taking" was the key to their success in the Promised Land. But I see something else. True, God was moving this group across the Jordan River to give them a land of their own. He wanted to give them something tangible—the words actually say to "take possession." But Joshua 1:15 states that God also wanted to give his people rest. *Rest* is defined as "freedom from activity or labor." In Moses' and Joshua's time, this rest was an earthly gift of peace and growth and provision found in the Promised Land. For Christians, this rest is a close, peaceful relationship with God that Christ has provided for us. We enter rest when we "take possession" of God's gift and "*make every effort* to enter that rest" (Hebrews 4:11, emphasis added).

Let's look at the how the Israelites made every effort to take possession of something God had and they wanted! A strong relationship with God was vital for them to experience soul strength. Words from the mouth of God breathed courage into Joshua's nostrils: "For the LORD your God will be with you wherever you go" (Joshua 1:9). Keep in mind that God knew the Israelites' weakness of heart and their tendency toward fuss and anxiety. That's what made his words to them so deeply personal and powerful. A whole and healthy Joshua did not question God's promise. Nor did the Israelites. They heard God's promise to stay close to them, and they ran with it!

The first chapter of Joshua gives us three vital insights that can help strengthen our relationship with the King:

1. Know God's character. In our highly sophisticated society, we are taught to test and challenge every piece of information we receive, including Scripture. Although this is not always a bad practice, we can, in our self-centered thinking, devise our own "world" and overlook the very character of God. We can even disregard God's promise that he is with us wherever we go. As a result, we become a people who are led not by a personal God, but by our own distrust, cynicism, and need to be in control. When we recognize God's thoughts and concerns, we know his character, and this brings us to a place of truth and rest.

2. Respond in the freedom he has given us. If your friend told you she would go on a walk with you in a couple of hours, and you questioned her word, you would not have rest. If you called your friend during those two hours to see if she was still going on the walk, you would be squelching the freedom of your friendship. You would be acting out of insecurity, rather than trusting your friend's commitment to you.

Good relationships give freedom. Relating well to God means that we recognize his character and interact with him based on what we know of him. When we relate well to God, it is always a response to his healthy and freeing way of relating to us. In the book of Joshua and throughout most of the Old Testament, God initiated relationship with his people. God relates to us in the same way today—as the initiator—and we have the freedom to join him or rebel against him. God's Will, his Logos, the Word, was up and running before time began, and he still moves forcefully throughout the universe. This eternal and forever God initiates a relationship with us, and we become intimate with him when we respond in the freedom he offers.

3. Make every effort to move toward God. Like Moses, we are forbidden to enter the land of rest when we live in unbelief—in other words, when we don't move toward God. James 4:8 says, "Draw near to God and He will draw near to you" (NASB). If we are moving toward God in our journeys, we move from strength to strength (see Psalm 84:7). If we aren't moving from strength to strength, we stagnate—we don't move at all. God is the One who initiates our moving from one strength to another. Our part is to respond. It's our response in our neediest moments that reveals the most about our relationship with God. As Mother Teresa once said, "We must have a real living determination to reach holiness." But what does that determination look like?

TAKING IT IN

7. Read Joshua 1:7-9 and 16 again, then summarize these verses in your own words.

8. How did Joshua communicate God's commands to the people? What was the people's response?

⊅ 9. Describe one area of your life in which you sense that God is commanding you to move. For example, does your child need more consistent discipline and attention from you? Do you need to break your addiction to drugs, pornography, or sex? Are you hesitant to make a long-term commitment in a relationship? For the remainder of this exercise, use verses 7-9 and 16 to speak truth into your "move."

10. What do the phrases "depart from your mouth" and "meditate" bring to mind (verse 8)?

11. These verses from Joshua 1 contain several action words for our hearts, minds, and souls. List the verbs (and verb phrases) from these verses. Next to each verb on your list, write a short prayer asking God for guidance and wisdom to follow through on the command. For example, next to the verb "turn" (verse 7) I might write, *Lord, show me how my mind turns from your Word during the day. Please remind me to turn to you and your Word when I forget.*

Read Ephesians 6:12-17.

12. Does the idea of wearing the armor of God appeal to you? In what ways would putting on the armor of God remind you of his commitment to a relationship with you?

13. In what ways do you need to trust in God's character more right now? Take some time to pray Joshua 1:16 in response to Ephesians 6:10-11.

MEDITATING ON GOD'S CHARACTER

The great diseases of our day are anxiety and depression. It's likely that you or someone you know struggles with spiritual unrest. Depression and anxiety are most definitely physical and mental illnesses. For many people, prescriptions for depression are a form of God's grace and mercy. Just as some people suffer from diabetes, others suffer from low serotonin levels, and God can provide healing through medicine. Depression and anxiety also come, however, when we move away from looking to God and his Word as our source of rest and instead find our primary satisfaction in work, material possessions, perfectionism, and independence. None of these things gives our souls true rest or freedom.

Joshua 1 and Ephesians 6:10-17 use similar language. Joshua 1:15 says that the Lord God would give the Israelites "rest," which is translated "to settle." This is not a leisurely kind of rest or a physical vacation. God wanted to give his people a home, a land with boundaries, safety, and food. I believe that's true for us in the spiritual realm as well. When Paul wrote about Christians standing firm (see Ephesians 6:14), he was speaking of a place of rest. This is a place where we humbly put ourselves in a position to receive God's gifts: the belt of truth, the shield of faith, the breastplate of righteousness, the helmet of salvation, the shoes of peace, and the sword of the Spirit. So how do we receive these gifts from the Lord

God? Do we *want* to receive rest? We need to know—not just intellectu-ally, but in a way that moves our hearts and desires—that God initiates relationship with us as a lover initiates relationship with the beloved.

St. John of the Cross wrote that "every quality or virtue that the Spirit really produces in our souls has three distinguishing characteristics...tran-quility, gentleness and strength."[1] When the soul chooses to move on its own, it cannot go far before running into despair and emptiness. When our souls respond to God's commands to "not let this Book of the Law depart from your mouth; meditate on it day and night" (Joshua 1:8), our hungers and addictions are replaced with a longing for God.

The word *meditate* in the Hebrew is *hagah,* which literally means "to mutter." Putting on the full armor of God means meditating on—mut-tering—the truth about who we are and who God is. When we stop med-itating on God's character and begin to murmur continually about our ambition, independence, and self-direction, we end up talking ourselves out of crossing the Jordan, receiving God's gifts, and conquering our ene-mies. To combat those self-centered murmurings (which for me start the moment I wake up in the morning), we must fill our mouths and our minds with reminders such as, "I will be with you wherever you go," "Be strong and courageous," "No one will be able to stand against you."

When we meditate on God's character, we are free to trust him, rest-ing in his commitment to a forever relationship with us. God wanted the Israelites to mutter his thoughts, to know and feel his presence, and to open their hands to receive his gifts. They responded with excitement and obedience because they knew his character. God wants us to respond the same way today. It is a free soul who can say to the Creator, "All that you command me I will do, and wherever you send me I will go."

---

1. St. John of the Cross, quoted in Evelyn Underhill, *The Spiritual Life* (Harrisburg, Pa.: Morehouse, 1985).

MAKING IT REAL

When Anne Bradstreet wrote this poem in the 1600s, she had recently moved from her aristocratic home in England to a more modest home in America. Although she was in difficult circumstances in a culture that was not her own, her poetry reveals what she chose to meditate on.

"CONTEMPLATIONS" BY ANNE BRADSTREET[2]

The trees all richly clad, yet void of pride,
Were gilded o'er by his rich golden head.
Their leaves and fruits seem'd painted but was true
Of green, of red, of yellow, mixed hue,
Rapt were my senses at this delectable view.

I wist not what to wish, yet sure thought I,
If so much excellence abide below,
How excellent is he that dwells on high?
Whose power and beauty by his works we know.
Sure he is goodness, wisdom, glory, light,
That hath this under world so richly dight.
More Heaven than Earth was here, no winter and no night.

Anne Bradstreet *chose* to meditate on God's character and his creation, confessing her worship-filled attitude. She *chose* to be secure in who God is. She didn't just "think positively," she thought about God's character—and that is real worship. Note that she doesn't say anything about what God has *done* for her; rather, she is filled with rapture at who he *is*.

---

2. Anne Bradstreet, "Contemplations," *Several Poems,* 2nd ed. (Boston: John Foster, 1678).

14. How do you think contemplating God's character ("Sure he is goodness, wisdom, glory, light…") draws us closer to him and helps us trust him more? Do you feel secure or insecure in your relationship with God and his character? Explain.

15. Describe a time when your senses were "rapt"—as the poet's were—in contemplation of creation.

16. Pay special attention this week to your meditations or "mutterings" about God. What do your thoughts about God reveal about your relationship with him?

THREE

TEARING OFF SELF-SUFFICIENCY

Picking Up the Shield of Faith

JOSHUA 2; EPHESIANS 6:12,16

*Behold the proud, his soul is not upright in him; but the just
shall live by his faith.*

—HABAKKUK 2:4, NKJV

Seven or eight miles from the swollen Jordan River lies the oldest city on
earth—Jericho. In biblical times Jericho controlled the important trade
route running the length of the Jordan Valley, as well as access to the hill
country of Canaan from the east. In its entirety, the city, stretching out
over seven acres, was a very strong fortress built to resist siege.

During the time of Joshua, when winter was turning to spring, the city
of Jericho was shut tight. Communication from inside or outside the walls
of the city was at a standstill. Jericho was bolted and barred because word
was out about the Israelites' God. But think about this: It wasn't an attack,

a seige, or a raid that sealed the doom of Jericho that spring. It was words—spoken, powerful, faith-full human words—that took Jericho down.

BREAKING GROUND

Do you ever find yourself manipulating conversations to receive praise from others? Do you ever protect yourself from relational intimacy by being emotionally detached and raising walls that distance you from others? Explain.

THE WALLS OF PRIDE

When we are proud, we work hard to gain applause from others. Literally and symbolically, the walls of Jericho were a tremendous source of pride and protection for this heathen city; its inhabitants were a proud and self-sufficient people. The people of Jericho, the Amorites, relied on the city's walls to separate them from and elevate them above the surrounding cultures. But their silence exposed their fear of the Israelites' God.

Immorality was the norm in Jericho, and people served gods that were not gods. The sin of these people had finally reached its full measure (see Genesis 15:16). The time for redemption had passed. Yet in Jericho itself lived a prostitute named Rahab, a woman whose words would bring down the proud city. It's in this next scene of the Joshua story that self-sufficiency—pride—and faith meet.

Read Joshua 2.

FIRST LOOKS

1. In a few sentences, summarize the scenes in this chapter.

2. Describe the setting. Who are the main characters? Who is the antagonist—the bad guy?

3. How would you compare the spirit of Jericho's community in this chapter with the spirit of Israel in Joshua 1?

4. On what did Rahab base her confident speech (verses 9-13)?

5. What information did the spies receive that encouraged them in their mission?

6. What words did Rahab and the spies use that indicated a greater concern for the communities they represented than for themselves?

Read Ephesians 6:12,16.

7. Using a dictionary, define the words *wrestle* (NKJV) and *faith*.

8. Who are a Christian's enemies?

9. In light of Ephesians 6, with whom is the king of Jericho ultimately wrestling in Joshua 2?

SPEAKING IN FAITH

The historian Josephus maintained that Rahab was an innkeeper in an unfavorable sense. Some people raise their eyebrows because the main character in this scene sold her body for sex in a corrupt, pagan culture. That's what she did, and that's what Jericho was. But this same Rahab earned a place in the book of Hebrews as a woman of great faith "because she welcomed the spies" (11:31). Ironically, this faith-full woman whom God would use to bring down Jericho lived in a house that was "on the city wall" (Joshua 2:15, NKJV)—the very wall that gave the Amorites a sense of strength and infallibility.

When the king's men, using fear-full human words, came to Rahab and told her to turn over the two Israelite spies at her establishment, her ears perked up. Rahab had heard about the Israelites from the Far Eastern and Middle Eastern men she entertained, and these rumors had fueled the king's fears. Rahab used the information she had, and choosing to protect the two spies in her charge, she sent the king's men in a different direction in hot pursuit of the spies. Rahab had heard the voices of fear, but she responded in faith to the words of truth about the Israelites and their God. I like that she didn't panic.

After the king's men left, Rahab and the spies spoke to one another in an other-worldly language, and we can see how their physical and spiritual worlds came together. At this point in the Joshua story, the Israelites had not received the land…yet. But faith is believing in things unseen. The dialogue between Rahab and the spies is spiritual, earthy, and honest. I think a bit of heaven comes to earth when we faith-fully speak truth to one another about what is seen to us but *unseen* to others. The spies learned from Rahab that the people of Jericho "melted" in fear when they heard that the two Amorite kings Sihon and Og were "completely destroyed" (Joshua 2:10-11). Rahab received affirmation from the spies that their God was active and powerful. Rahab and the spies used spoken human words to lift their shields of faith—to act out of the faith they had. It was precisely at that moment that things began to happen for Rahab and the spies—and things began to fall apart for the king of Jericho! The faith of Rahab and the spies gave them strength and courage.

Rahab's deceptive response to the king's men was her way of verbally and physically turning from her pagan culture. Though she was surrounded by the eight-foot-wide city walls and life was going on as usual,

Rahab did the unthinkable: She believed. Rahab had faith in the power and truth of words—they were evidence to her of a living God.

In the midst of a battle, Rahab made a decision to go against the evil surrounding her. We, too, have times in our lives when we have to *choose* God's strategies over our own. At those times, our spiritual and physical worlds collide. Our proud souls no longer stand upright, and we begin responding to the powerful, faith-full words spoken to us by God's agents.

Read Joshua 2 and Ephesians 6:12,16 again.

✄ TAKING IT IN

10. Look for word patterns in the Joshua narrative. What phrases or words are repeated?

11. Describe the scene in Joshua 2.

Background information:

Complication (conflict):

Crisis or turning point (climax):

Falling action and resolution:

12. What words describe the tone or mood of this scene?

13. Plot and character are often inseparable. As readers we come to
care about, identify with, and judge the characters of this story.
Imagine the dialogue between Rahab and Joshua's spies.
Observe their actions. Listen to what they said and how they
said it. Look for clues and connections that will help you understand these characters, then, in the space below, compare the
character of Rahab with the character of the spies.

The Spies   *Rahab*

WORDS OF FAITH

We see in Scripture that God commands his strength when we lift our
shield of faith and ask him to act (see Psalm 68:28). Even when my faith
is weak, I must lift what I have. I must say what I know. Not all of me is
fully persuaded that God can be trusted all the time—and admitting that
to God exposes my pride. In other words, I'm still wrestling with my flesh,
the powers of darkness, and the things of this world! I struggle so much
with pride because it sometimes looks and feels like faith.

But it's in my weakest moments when I speak all I know that faith carries me to the threshold of strength. And that's the point: It doesn't matter that our faith is flimsy and weak. God's shield of faith is always there for us. As Elizabeth Goudge writes in *Gentian Hill,* "Every man has within him a store of strength, both physical and spiritual, of which he is utterly unaware until the moment of crisis.... You can experience the reality of what you believe in only one way, by putting it to the test."[1]

The Greek word for "wrestle" (NKJV) or "struggle" in Ephesians 6:12 is *pale.* Beginning with Homer in 8 B.C., this word was used to describe a contest between two people in which each person endeavored to throw the other. The contest was decided when the victor was able to press and hold down his opponent with a hand on his neck. God gives us the strength we need to wrestle with our fears and pride and to hold them down. We need to see that we are wrestling for a purpose; it's a good fight.

Both Rahab and the spies had a fight on their hands. In their story we see them wrestling with two enemies, both of which were a form of pride.

Rahab's enemy was her self-consciousness. Rahab was very aware of her low position as a call girl and innkeeper. She could have been so self-conscious—so proud in the sense of being anxious about who she was—that she wouldn't have been able to offer anything to the spies. Instead, she moved beyond her pride and had faith that God could use her to wrestle the powers of darkness in her city.

Rahab represents any of us who wrestle with sin and temptation in the presence of the Creator. We feel self-conscious because we know our own thoughts and behaviors. Self-consciousness births seeds of pride because we are focusing on ourselves and refusing to recognize how God sees us through Christ. Pride turns us back to a dead-end self, but God's weapon of faith does not allow us to stay in that self-conscious place because faith moves us up and out to confidence in him.

The spies' enemy was their self-righteousness. The spies were aware of

---

1. Elizabeth Goudge, *Gentian Hill* (London: Coronet Books, 1965), 141.

their high position as FBI agents for the Most High God. But when they were forced to rely on a woman of low position for protection and confirmation of their mission, the spies' cloak of superiority vanished. Their faith quickly changed to an earthy God-didn't-choose-us-because-we're-the-golden-boys kind of faith.

Self-consciousness and self-righteousness are two sides of the same coin: self. With the former we're deflated, and with the latter we're puffed up. In either case, it's pride. Rahab's faith began when she wrestled with her pride, held it down with her hand on its neck, and hid the spies. The spies' faith was strengthened when they heard the words Rahab spoke—"I know that the LORD has given this land to you.... [He] is God in heaven above and on the earth below." (verses 9,11)—and they responded with faith—"*When* the Lord gives us the land" (verse 14, emphasis added). It was words—spoken human words, true eternal words—that brought faith.

When God wants us to leave the old and enter the new, whether geographically, relationally, emotionally, or spiritually, he commands his strength so that we can fight the Enemy. In this new place we want to stand for the unseen against the seen, we expect spiritual warfare, and we are willing to suffer loss. We need to respond with what we already know, even if our faith is small and weak. Christ answered the disciples' question about their failure when he said to them, "If you have faith as small as a mustard seed, *you can say to this mountain, 'Move from here to there' and it will move*" (Matthew 17:20, emphasis added).

We need to be encouraged if we are to be persons of soul strength, and much of our courage depends on words such as "The LORD has given this land to you." Do we encourage one another enough with words like these? As Christians, we need a tremendous amount of spoken encouragement to help us lift the shield of faith and believe that God will make us victorious in our battles.

As Rahab's faith was growing, the plot and pride of Jericho began to unravel. At the same time, Joshua's officers were speaking the words "Be strong and courageous" at the Israelite camp seven miles away. While the spirit of the Israelite community was thriving, the people of Jericho were melting in fear. The Israelites were gaining strength through God's words and pinning down their fears; the people of Jericho were losing their courage because of their pride and lack of faith.

A Story of Faith

My Jewish mother says that God used words, the spoken words of an unlikely woman, to cut to her heart and bring her to faith in Christ. My mother is the youngest daughter of Ruth and Samuel Goldstein, a Jewish couple who created a good life for their three children in Philadelphia after World War I. Samuel was the owner of a tailor shop in downtown Philadelphia until mental illness debilitated both him and his business. Afraid of what would happen to her children, Ruth placed them with Jewish foster families until she earned enough money on her own to bring them home. When the children came back into Ruth's life, they were reintroduced to a large extended Jewish family who faithfully observed Yom Kippur and Hanukkah, but who did not always provide the love and emotional response the children needed. My mother tells me that through all the Hebrew lessons and bar mitzvahs, through the separation from her parents and her two older brothers, through the fighting with her unstable mother, she knew there was a God who was real.

Years later, after my mother met and married my father, she heard the words that ripped her to the core. A woman in her neighborhood who struggled with alcoholism looked my mother in the eyes and said, "Life is tough, and there's only one way to live it—through faith in Jesus Christ." Shocked and full of pride, my mother said to her, "How can you say this to a Jewish woman?"

"It's the only way to live this life," the woman responded.

Believing that Jesus is Lord meant my mother had to die to everything she had ever known: her previous perspective, her childhood, her future plans, her attachments to Jewish tradition. But those words—those faithfull, human words—would not leave her. A few years later she found herself on her knees confessing with her mouth that Jesus Christ is God. Her journey of faith in Christ meant the death of her self-conscious pride as a Jew. She embraced God as never before. She had a faith that was desperately personal.

Like Rahab and the spies, like so many of us, my mother heard faithfull words and chose to wrestle with her pride so she herself could have faith and receive the strength of God.

✎ MAKING IT REAL

More than two hundred years ago, hymn writer and Methodist pastor John Wesley formed a group of people who met regularly to keep one another accountable—to dismantle pride in their lives and to raise their shields of faith. We don't know much about this "Holy Club," but we can benefit from its purpose. Below are twenty-two questions the members of John Wesley's Holy Club asked themselves each day in their devotions.

"A TEST FOR SELF-EXAMINATION" BY JOHN WESLEY

1. Am I consciously or unconsciously creating the impression that I am better than I really am? In other words, am I a hypocrite?
2. Am I honest in all my acts and words or do I exaggerate?
3. Do I confidentially pass on to others what was told to me in confidence?
4. Can I be trusted?
5. Am I a slave to dress, friends, work, or habits?
6. Am I self-conscious, self-pitying, or self-justifying?
7. Did the Bible live in me today?
8. Do I give the Bible time to speak to me every day?

9. Am I enjoying prayer?

10. When did I last speak to someone else of my faith?

11. Do I pray about the money I spend?

12. Do I get to bed on time; and get up on time?

13. Do I disobey God in anything?

14. Do I insist upon doing something about which my conscience is uneasy?

15. Am I defeated in any part of my life?

16. Am I jealous, impure, critical, irritable, touchy, or distrustful?

17. How do I spend my spare time?

18. Am I proud?

19. Do I thank God that I am not as other people, especially as the Pharisee who despised the publican?

20. Is there anyone whom I fear, dislike, disown, criticize, hold resentment toward or disregard? If so, what am I doing about it?

21. Do I grumble or complain constantly?

22. Is Christ real to me?

14. With what kind of pride do you struggle most: self-conscious pride or self-righteous pride? Explain.

15. Which of Wesley's questions made you stop and think the most? Why? How do Wesley's questions help you lift your shield of faith and fight against pride?

FOUR

Revealing
What Is

Putting On the Belt of Truth

Joshua 3–4; Ephesians 6:13-14;
Psalm 46:10

*The brain, when it is disengaged from the heart, turns
vicious. (Conversely, the heart, when it is disengaged from
the brain, can become sentimental and untruthful.)*
—Madeleine L'Engle, *Madeleine L'Engle Herself*

Oregon's rugged terrain spreads from the rocky coast to a beautiful moun-
tainous region 140 miles to the east. Living in the Willamette Valley is a
privilege given us by the pioneers who settled here 125 years ago. Roads
and highways feel somehow out of place; I wonder at times if human
beings were meant to exist here considering the tremendous risks the original pioneers took. On a clear day, as I drive down into the lush valley that

stretches from Mount Hood to the coast, I think about Annie Dillard's book *The Living,* in which she writes about the early pioneers of the Pacific Northwest who faced death on a daily basis. It seemed that human life in this part of the country was not meant to be, but the pioneers were intent on making a new life in what many called the land flowing with milk and honey. My analytical and cynical mind screams out to those pioneers, *Go back! Who cares that your former lives were too simple or unproductive? Why would you choose to wrestle death?*

But now, years later, I dwell in a land where mountains and clouds and rain and sun dance together, exalting the rugged beauty of the Creator—and I couldn't see that dance on the East Coast. I am grateful to those who went before me and for the earnestness with which they told their stories, but what fueled their imaginations is a mystery to me. How did they know it would all work out?

Like the early pioneers with their strong sense of calling, Joshua and Paul were intimately involved with moving and journeying from the old to the new. Both were cultured visionaries in charge of a group of people. Joshua was a military leader who followed Moses and led the Israelites the rest of the way through the desert to the Promised Land. Paul was a missionary who spoke and wrote and preached on how to spiritually leave the old life for the new life in Christ. Both Joshua and Paul pioneered where it seemed life was not meant to be. Because they retold their stories with both their heads and hearts, we catch a glimpse of who they were and who God is. This truth telling, this storytelling, is what Augustine called "the affirmation of what is."

When Paul wrote about buckling "the belt of truth" around our waists, he was referring to this idea of knowing who God is and who we are. When we know these truths, we can stand strong.

Breaking Ground

Recall a time in your life when God revealed his character and yours through an amazing circumstance. Tell the story.

Read Joshua 3–4.

First Looks

1. What event does this passage describe? When did this event happen (4:19)?

2. What instructions were given to the people for the coming events (3:3–4:12)?

3. What event is at the center of these activities? Look at Exodus 37:1-9 and Deuteronomy 10:1-5. Describe this intimate symbol and its contents.

4. How does the way in which this story is told (think about the pattern of words, the word tense, and the order of the telling of the events) influence our reading of this narrative?

5. According to Joshua 3:10, what kind of God did Joshua say the people would "know"? Why is this significant?

6. What are the two main ceremonies in these chapters?

Knowing God

Joshua 3 and 4 can be confusing because they are written with an interplay of word and action rather than in chronological order. One commentator sees these two chapters as a composite of various traditions woven together and suggests that they represent an ancient liturgy in which a Jordan "crossing" was symbolically enacted in ceremony. Regardless of the style in which these chapters were written, the stories themselves offer us rich insight into why God led his people on a specific journey to know him: He wanted them to see that *what* they did for truth was just as important as *how* they did it. From this amazing story, we discover a three-tiered process of knowing truth.

1. Know God with your head. What was about to happen was a miracle. Joshua stated that, by this miracle, the Israelites would "know" the living God (3:10). The Hebrew word *yada,* translated "to know," means "an experiential knowing, a perception of truth in a very practical way." In 3:13, Joshua verbalized what the reality *would* be—the priests who carried "the ark of the LORD—the Lord of all the earth" would cause the waters to "stand in a heap." It's intellectually tempting for us to analyze how waters could stand up or why the priest's feet held so much power. Head knowledge of God is a start toward truly knowing him, but by itself, it's not enough.

2. Know God with your head and your heart. The events of chapter 4 of the Joshua story easily follow chapter 3. They actually took place just a few minutes after the Israelites had crossed the Jordan River. When the people had crossed over, Joshua wasted no time giving orders to erect a memorial to God's faithfulness to them. While representatives from each tribe were heaving giant-size stones out of the Jordan, Joshua explained why they were doing this. The reason for setting up a memorial was of such great importance that Joshua told the people that they should tell future generations about how they had crossed over the Jordan on dry ground (see 4:20-24).

We must not downplay the significance of what the crossing means to us today by saying, "Well, that's what God did in Bible times." We must read this history, this true story, for exactly what it is! As readers, we should enter into the facts and the feelings as if we were watching the plot of a movie unfold. Do we see the truth this narrative reveals about the Israelites and about God? Once we know a God-story with our heads and hearts, we can then tell it the same way.

3. Make God known with your head and your heart. The word *tell* comes from the Hebrew word *hoda tem* meaning "to cause to know." This word is from the root word *yada* meaning "to know." It is an experiential knowing, a knowing with both head and heart at the same time.

The living God, the God of all the earth, wanted the Israelites to know him with both their heads and their hearts. Then, simply, he wanted them to transfer that precious gift of "knowing" to their children. It was not just the facts that the Israelites were to pass along. When they retold this story, they were to retell it with passion, with a you know, you know, you know—*yada, yada, yada.*

TAKING IT IN

7. In Joshua 3 and 4, underline the phrase "crossed over" each time you read it, and circle the phrases "stand" or "stand firm." Why do you think the author repeated these words or phrases?

✐ 8. In what artistic form could these two chapters be expressed? As you read them, what art form comes to your mind? Dance? Music? Painting? Something else?

9. How would the Israelites' retelling of the Jordan crossing and the erecting of a memorial solidify their head and heart knowledge of the Most High God?

10. Read Psalm 68:11 and 25. Based on Israel's tradition of celebration, what sounds and activities might have characterized the Jordan crossing?

Read Ephesians 6:13-14 and Psalm 46:10.

11. How do "standing firm" and "being still" help you "know" God?

12. In what area(s) of your life do you need to know God? Ask God to help you stand firm and be still (translated "be limp") so that you can know his power in that area today.

A GENTLE REALITY

On our journey to soul strength, one of the most difficult skills to learn is to listen when God reveals the truth about an area in our lives that he wants to change. As I've learned more about the truth of God's character, the truth of who I am has emerged, and in the light of this truth, God has begun to strengthen my soul.

Last summer it became obvious that I could not control my anger. At times my outrage would be so sudden that it took me by surprise, and I wondered where the anger came from. Anger has always fueled parts of my personality, but I knew something was wrong when my feelings were so intense. Around this time I had been asking God to reveal to me the materials I was using to build on his foundation. Was I using "gold, silver, costly stones, wood, hay or straw" (1 Corinthians 3:12)? I knew that one day I will stand before him, and my work will be shown for what it is.

I was not prepared for what God revealed to me. Not long after this time of seeking, I became keenly aware of the anger and frustrations I prayerfully brought to his throne. It's not that God wasn't accepting me as I was, but he wanted me to get rid of my anger. With characteristic moxie and in my East Coast, passionate way, I began working hard to get rid of this root of bitterness in my heart. I prayed hard, studied even harder, disciplined my time, talked openly about my sin, and genuinely thought I was doing all the right things.

A few months later I found myself extremely uptight and frustrated in a situation that didn't really call for that much frustration. I put myself in a room away from other people and pleaded with God to help me. The image that came to my mind was a large fruit tree planted smack in the middle of my heart. Because I could not remove the anger myself, the seeds of my frustrations only nurtured its growth, producing a tree with bitter fruit. Minor frustrations seemed enormous as I reached over to pluck a piece of fruit off my bitterness tree, which usually resulted in my lashing out at someone I love. As I saw this image, not only did I have a sense of defeat in my personal relationships, but I was humiliated in God's presence—where could I go from here? The real me had emerged, and the truth of it all seemed daunting.

This is where the second part of truth—who *God* is—became for me an intimate, gentle reality. I dared not put one foot out of bed until I whispered, "Oh, God, have mercy on me and fill me with your Holy Spirit." With the truth of who I was standing in stark contrast to the truth of Scripture, it became obvious that God himself would have to remove that tree of anger.

I am very drawn to God's passion, his displeasure with injustice, and his sometimes dramatic ways of communicating with those who love him, and my anger took a turn toward those things. Soon after I prayed about the image of the tree, I called out to God during a time of anger and worked very hard to be still, to stand firm. Within minutes I felt his gentleness clothe my spirit; I was able to control my anger. Just as certain pieces of music can move my soul like nothing else, certain aspects of God's character do the same for me, releasing me from tension. I know who I am, and, on a very small scale, I've learned who God is. These two truths buckled around my waist give my soul a deep and rich strength.

STILL STANDING

Immediately following the command to put on the full armor of God, Paul used the Greek word *ergazomai*. We read it as "hav[ing] done everything, to stand" (Ephesians 6:13). The Greek word means "to effect by labor, to achieve, to work out, to bring about, to perform." Paul says that after we have worked hard to stand firm, to receive, to pause (you may want to reread the definition of *stand* in chapter 1), then we put on the specific pieces of his armor. Recognizing the Ephesians' battle with weakness,

Paul knew they were tempted to revert to their former lifestyle. By telling them to "stand firm," the apostle revealed a truth that had to be embraced before the Ephesians could find soul strength.

The truth is this: Without eagerness or vigilance, we become slothful. We must work hard at being watchful. Spiritually, we must watch over our entire being. We must particularly watch those areas where we are weakest. The Lord God knew his people were weak in the knowledge of who he was, so he parted the waters, but they had to walk through. He also merged the waters together again, and the people memorialized this act with backbreaking stones. God created a situation that demanded eagerness and vigilance, and as a result, the head and heart knowledge that God revealed to the Israelites was now part of them! It's really quite brilliant. Where in your life does it seem impossible for God to work? Are you eager to do everything you must do to stand firm?

In the Joshua story we see how the Israelites crossed the Jordan and how they labored to erect the memorial stones. Immediately following these two events, Joshua gave them their next directive: "Tell the story." Imagine the creative emotional energy of 2.5 million people that pumped, primed, and permeated everything they saw. The "telling" of the story was a form of self-expression that satisfied the musicians, the artists, the dramatists, the writers, the creative souls. At its best, creativity reveals truth, reveals reality, reveals what is. But how do we "tell the story" in our own lives? How do we live with the belt of truth around our waists? To answer these questions, we must look at the dual purpose of the belt of truth.

1. *The truth about who we are.* Buckling truth around your waist means to be honest about who you are in your inner person. In Joshua 3 and 4, each character or set of characters had a role to play in the Jordan-crossing, the stone-erecting, and the child-telling scenes. In Joshua 3, the Israelites were told to move out from their positions and follow the priests who were carrying the ark of the Lord. "Then," Joshua explained,

"you will know which way to go, since you have never been this way before" (3:4).

Each of us is meant to follow someone. When we know who we are, we know whom to follow. We must follow hard after truth, knowing that our "descendants" are following after us (see Joshua 4:21). We must know how we really think and feel; we must understand our true character and the way we make choices. How does one do this without thinking too much about oneself? This is where our efforts, our vigilance should be focused on knowing God's truth.

2. The truth of God's Word. We must immerse ourselves in right doctrine and theology, and in love for God and his church. A Christian's truth is that Jesus Christ is the very center of reality. He is real and he is alive. In Joshua 4, we read that God "dried up the Jordan" so that "all the peoples of the earth might know that the hand of the LORD is powerful" (verses 23-24). As followers of God, we need to work hard at discovering what God has done.

These two truths—who we are and who God is—form the buckled belt around our waists. At the time Paul wrote Ephesians, soldiers wore a padded doublet (or belt) lined with satin under their armor. The mail skirt was tied to the points or the laces that hung from the doublet. Without the doublet underneath the mail skirt, the armor was incomplete. Without the truth of who we are and who God is, the armor we need for soul strength is incomplete.

William Gurnall, a seventeenth-century Puritan pastor who wrote *The Christian in Complete Armour,* wrote this about truth: "Truth in the heart is an exact copy of truth in God's word—they agree as a face in the mirror corresponds to the face of a man who looks into it. Therefore, if truth in the word is harmonious, then truth in the heart, which is nothing but the impression of it, must be also."[1]

---

1. William Gurnall, June 18th devotional, "The Sincere Soul Shows Its Simplicity" in *The Christian in Complete Armour* (Carlisle, Pa.: Banner of Truth, 1996).

MAKING IT REAL

Still not convinced you need to know the truth about yourself? Wait until you read this story about a woman who sought everything but truth!

"THE DIAMOND NECKLACE" BY GUY DE MAUPASSANT[2]

She was one of those pretty, charming young ladies, born, as if through an error of destiny, into a family of clerks. She had no dowry, no hopes, no means of becoming known, appreciated, loved, and married by a man either rich or distinguished; and she allowed herself to marry a petty clerk in the office of the Board of Education.

She was simple, not being able to adorn herself; but she was unhappy, as one out of her class; for women belong to no caste, no race; their grace, their beauty, and their charm serving them in the place of birth and family. Their inborn finesse, their instinctive elegance, their suppleness of wit are their only aristocracy, making some daughters of the people the equal of great ladies.

She suffered incessantly, feeling herself born for all delicacies and luxuries. She suffered from the poverty of her apartment, the shabby walls, the worn chair, and the faded stuffs. All these things, which another woman of her station would not have noticed, tortured and angered her. The sight of the little Breton, who made this humble home, awoke in her sad regrets and desperate dreams. She thought of quiet antechambers, with their Oriental hangings, lighted by high, bronze torches, and of the two great footmen in short trousers who sleep in the large armchairs, made sleepy by the heavy air from the heating apparatus. She thought of large drawing-rooms, hung in old silks, of graceful pieces of furniture carrying bric-à-brac of inestimable value, and of the little perfumed coquettish apartments, made for five o'clock chats

---

2. Guy de Maupassant, "The Diamond Necklace" in *The Works of Guy de Maupassant* (Roslyn, N.Y.: Black's Readers Service, 1903), 28-33.

with most intimate friends, men known and sought after, whose attention all women envied and desired.

When she seated herself for dinner, before the round table where the tablecloth had been used three days, opposite her husband, who uncovered the tureen with a delighted air, saying: "Oh! [T]he good potpie! I know nothing better than that—" she would think of the elegant dinners, of the shining silver, of the tapestries peopling the walls with ancient personages and rare birds in the midst of fairy forests; she thought of the exquisite food served on marvelous dishes, of the whispered gallantries, listened to with the smile of the sphinx, while eating the rose-colored flesh of the trout or a chicken's wing.

She had neither frocks nor jewels, nothing. And she loved only those things. She felt that she was made for them. She had such a desire to please, to be sought after, to be clever, and courted.

She had a rich friend, a schoolmate at the convent, whom she did not like to visit, she suffered so much when she returned. And she wept for whole days from chagrin, from regret, from despair, and disappointment.

One evening her husband returned elated, bearing in his hand a large envelope.

"Here," he said, "here is something for you."

She quickly tore open the wrapper and drew out a printed card on which were inscribed these words:

The Minister of Public Instruction and Madame George Ramponneau
ask the honor of Monsieur and Madame Loisel's company Monday
evening, January 18, at the Minister's residence.

Instead of being delighted, as her husband had hoped, she threw the invitation spitefully upon the table murmuring:

"What do you suppose I want with that?"

"But, my dearie, I thought it would make you happy. You never go out, and this is an occasion, and a fine one! I had a great deal of trouble to get it. Everybody wishes one, and it is very select; not many are given to employees. You will see the whole official world there."

She looked at him with an irritated eye and declared impatiently:

"What do you suppose I have to wear to such a thing as that?"

He had not thought of that; he stammered:

"Why, the dress you wear when we go to the theater. It seems very pretty to me—"

He was silent, stupefied, in dismay, at the sight of his wife weeping. Two great tears fell slowly from the corners of his eyes toward the corners of his mouth; he stammered:

"What is the matter? What is the matter?"

By a violent effort, she had controlled her vexation and responded in a calm voice, wiping her moist cheeks:

"Nothing. Only I have no dress and consequently I cannot go to this affair. Give your card to some colleague whose wife is better fitted out than I."

He was grieved, but answered:

"Let us see, Matilda. How much would a suitable costume cost, something that would serve for other occasions, something very simple?"

She reflected for some seconds, making estimates and thinking of a sum that she could ask for without bringing with it an immediate refusal and a frightened exclamation from the economical clerk.

Finally she said, in a hesitating voice:

"I cannot tell exactly, but it seems to me that four hundred francs ought to cover it."

He turned a little pale, for he had saved just this sum to buy a gun that he might be able to join some hunting parties the next summer, on the plains of Nanterre, with some friends who went to shoot larks up there on Sunday. Nevertheless, he answered:

"Very well. I will give you four hundred francs. But try to have a pretty dress."

☙◦❧

The day of the ball approached and Madame Loisel seemed sad, disturbed, anxious. Nevertheless, her dress was nearly ready. Her husband said to her one evening:

"What is the matter with you? You have acted strangely for two or three days."

And she responded: "I am vexed not to have a jewel, not one stone, nothing to adorn myself with. I shall have such a poverty-laden look. I would prefer not to go to this party."

He replied: "You can wear some natural flowers. At this season they look very *chic*. For ten francs you can have two or three magnificent roses."

She was not convinced. "No," she replied, "there is nothing more humiliating than to have a shabby air in the midst of rich women."

Then her husband cried out: "How stupid we are! Go and find your friend Madame Forestier and ask her to lend you her jewels. You are well enough acquainted with her to do this."

She uttered a cry of joy: "It is true!" she said. "I had not thought of that."

The next day she took herself to her friend's house and related her story of distress. Madame Forestier went to her closet with the glass doors, took out a large jewel-case, brought it, opened it, and said: "Choose, my dear."

She saw at first some bracelets, then a collar of pearls, then a Venetian cross of gold and jewels and of admirable workmanship. She tried the jewels before the glass, hesitated, but could neither decide to take them nor leave them. Then she asked:

"Have you nothing more?"

"Why, yes. Look for yourself. I do not know what will please you."

Suddenly she discovered, in a black satin box, a superb necklace of diamonds, and heart beat fast with an immoderate desire. Her hands trembled as she took them up. She placed them about her throat against her dress, and remained in ecstasy before them. Then she asked, in a hesitating voice, full of anxiety:

"Could you lend me this? Only this?"

"Why, yes, certainly."

She fell upon the neck of her friend, embraced her with passion, then went away with her treasure.

∽o∾

The day of the ball arrived. Madame Loisel was a great success. She was the prettiest of all, elegant, gracious, smiling, and full of joy. All the men noticed her, asked her name, and wanted to be presented. All the members of the Cabinet wished to waltz with her. The Minister of Education paid her some attention.

She danced with enthusiasm, with passion, intoxicated with pleasure, thinking of nothing, in the triumph of her beauty, in the glory of her success, in a kind of cloud of happiness that came of all this homage, and all this admiration, of all these awakened desires, and this victory so complete and sweet to the heart of woman.

She went home toward four o'clock in the morning. Her husband had been half asleep in one of the little salons since midnight, with three other gentlemen whose wives were enjoying themselves very much.

He threw around her shoulders the wraps they had carried for the coming home, modest garments of everyday wear, whose poverty clashed with the elegance of the ball costume. She felt this and wished to hurry away in order not to be noticed by the other women who were wrapping themselves in rich furs.

Loisel retained her: "Wait," said he. "You will catch cold out there. I am going to call a cab."

But she would not listen and descended the steps rapidly. When they were in the street, they found no carriage; and they began to seek for one, hailing the coachmen whom they saw at a distance.

They walked along toward the Seine, hopeless and shivering. Finally they found on the dock one of those old, nocturnal *coupés* that one sees in Paris after nightfall, as if they were ashamed of their misery by day.

It took them as far as their door in Martyr street, and they went wearily up to their apartment. It was all over for her. And on his part, he remembered that he would have to be at the office by ten o'clock.

She removed the wraps from her shoulders before the glass, for a final view of herself in her glory. Suddenly she uttered a cry. Her necklace was not around her neck.

Her husband, already half undressed, asked: "What is the matter?"

She turned toward him excitedly:

"I have—I have—I no longer have Madame Forestier's necklace."

He arose in dismay: "What! How is that? It is not possible."

And they looked in the folds of the dress, in the folds of the mantle, in the pockets, everywhere. They could not find it.

He asked: "You are sure you still had it when we left the house?"

"Yes, I felt it in the vestibule as we came out."

"But if you had lost it in the street, we should have heard it fall. It must be in the cab."

"Yes. It is probable. Did you take the number?"

"No. And you, did you notice what it was?"

"No."

They looked at each other utterly cast down. Finally, Loisel dressed himself again.

"I am going," said he, "over the track where we went on foot, to see if I can find it."

And he went. She remained in her evening gown, not having the force to go to bed, stretched upon a chair, without ambition or thoughts.

Toward seven o'clock her husband returned. He had found nothing.

He went to the police and to the cab offices, and put an advertisement in the newspapers, offering a reward; he did everything that afforded them a suspicion of hope.

She waited all day in a state of bewilderment before this frightful disaster. Loisel returned at evening with his face harrowed and pale; and had discovered nothing.

"It will be necessary," said he, "to write to your friend that you have broken the clasp of the necklace and that you will have it repaired. That will give us time to turn around."

She wrote as he dictated.

∽o∾

At the end of a week, they had lost all hope. And Loisel, older by five years, declared:

"We must take measures to replace this jewel."

The next day they took the box which had inclosed it, to the jeweler whose name was on the inside. He consulted his books:

"It is not I, Madame," said he, "who sold this necklace; I only furnished the casket."

Then they went from jeweler to jeweler seeking a necklace like the other one, consulting their memories, and ill, both of them, with chagrin and anxiety.

In a shop of the Palais-Royal, they found a chaplet of diamonds which seemed to them exactly like the one they had lost. It was valued at forty thousand francs. They could get it for thirty-six thousand.

They begged the jeweler not to sell it for three days. And they made an arrangement by which they might return it for thirty-four thousand francs if they found the other one before the end of February.

Loisel possessed eighteen thousand francs which his father had left him. He borrowed the rest.

He borrowed it, asking for a thousand francs of one, five hundred of another, five louis of this one, and three louis of that one. He gave notes, made ruinous promises, took money of usurers and the whole race of lenders He compromised his whole existence, in fact, risked his signature, without even knowing whether he could make it good or not, and, harassed by anxiety for the future, by the black misery which surrounded him, and by the prospect of all physical privations and moral torture, he went to get the new necklace, depositing on the merchant's counter thirty-six thousand francs.

When Madame Loisel took back the jewels to Madame Forestier, the latter said to her in a frigid tone:

"You should have returned them to me sooner, for I might have needed them."

She did not open the jewel-box as her friend feared she would. If she should perceive the substitution, what would she think? What should she say? Would she take her for a robber?

Madame Loisel now knew the horrible life of necessity. She did her part, however, completely, heroically. It was necessary to pay this frightful debt. She would pay it. They sent away the maid; they changed their lodgings; they rented some rooms under a mansard roof.

She learned the heavy cares of a household, the odious work of a kitchen. She washed the dishes, using her rosy nails upon the greasy pots and the bottoms of the stewpans. She washed the soiled linen, the chemises and dishcloths, which she hung on the line to dry; she took down the refuse to the street each morning and brought up the water, stopping at each landing to breathe. And, clothed like a woman of the people, she went to the grocer's, the butcher's, and the fruiterer's, with her basket on her arm, shopping, haggling to the last sou her miserable money.

Every month it was necessary to renew some notes, thus obtaining time, and to pay others.

The husband worked evenings, putting the books of some merchants in order, and nights he often did copying at five sous a page.

And this life lasted ten years.

At the end of ten years, they had restored all, all, with interest of the usurer, and accumulated interest besides.

Madame Loisel seemed old now. She had become a strong, hard woman, the crude woman of the poor household. Her hair badly dressed, her skirts awry, her hands red, she spoke in a loud tone, and washed the floors with large pails of water. But sometimes, when her husband was at the office, she would seat herself before the window and think of that evening party of former times, of that ball where she was so beautiful and so flattered.

How would it have been if she had not lost that necklace: Who knows? Who knows? How singular is life, and how full of changes! How small a thing will ruin or save one!

ॐ

One Sunday, as she was taking a walk in the Champs-Elysées to rid herself of the cares of the week, she suddenly perceived a woman walking with a child. It was Madame Forestier, still young, still pretty, still attractive. Madame Loisel was affected. Should she speak to her? Yes, certainly. And now that she had paid, she would tell her all. Why not?

She approached her. "Good morning, Jeanne."

Her friend did not recognize her and was astonished to be so familiarly addressed by this common personage. She stammered:

"But, Madame—I do not know—you must be mistaken—"

"No, I am Matilda Loisel."

Her friend uttered a cry of astonishment: "Oh! [M]y poor Matilda! How you have changed—"

"Yes, I have had some hard days since I saw you; and some miserable ones—and all because of you—"

"Because of me? How is that?"

"You recall the diamond necklace that you loaned me to wear to the Commissioner's ball?"

"Yes, very well."

"Well, I lost it."

"How is that, since you returned it to me?"

"I returned another to you exactly like it. And it has taken us ten years to pay for it. You can understand that it was not easy for us who have nothing. But it is finished and I am decently content."

Madame Forestier stopped short. She said:

"You say that you bought a diamond necklace to replace mine?"

"Yes. You did not perceive it then? They were just alike."

And she smiled with a proud and simple joy. Madame Forestier was touched and took both her hands as she replied:

"Oh! [M]y poor Matilda! Mine were false. They were not worth over five hundred francs!"

∽०∾

13. What truths about herself and her situation was the wife not willing to face? How might her life have been different had she listened to the truth?

14. Do you think the necklace disaster changed the wife for better or worse? Explain.

15. Do you have difficulty hearing the truth about yourself that God is speaking to your heart? Explain.

16. What areas in your life do you think God wants to change? What steps can you take to put on the belt of truth in order to know yourself and God more fully?

FIVE

MOVING FORWARD

Wearing the Breastplate of Righteousness and the Shoes of Peace

JOSHUA 5; EPHESIANS 6:14B-15

There is a way of ordering our mental life on more than one level at once. On one level we may be thinking, discussing, seeing, calculating, meeting all the demands of external affairs. But deep within, behind the scenes, at a profounder level, we may also be in prayer and adoration, song and worship and a gentle receptiveness to divine breathings.... Between these two levels is fruitful interplay, but ever the accent must be upon the deeper level, where the soul dwells in the presence of the Holy One.

—THOMAS KELLY, *A Testament of Devotion*

Just as objects are drawn to the surface or center of the earth by the force of gravity, I'm instinctively drawn to reading times with our daughters. When my entire lap is covered with small bodies, and the four of us are concentrating on the pictures in front of us, listening to the sound of language dancing in the air, the house is filled with peace and a sense of order. The moments prior to this settling down are often chaotic, tense, and frustrating for each of us. But once we're reading together, I truly believe that all is right with the world.

God's peace is prefaced with an order, a structure, that is his alone. Training, doing what is right, must take place first in order for peace to take root, like the "peaceful fruit of righteousness to those who have been trained by it" (Hebrews 12:11, NRSV). When we follow the order of God, he gives us peace of mind, peace of soul, and peace of spirit in the middle of our spiritual battles.

BREAKING GROUND

When was the last time you experienced a deep sense of well-being?

THE KISS OF PEACE

The primary and basic idea of peace is the Old Testament word *shalom*—completeness, soundness, wholeness. It's a favorite biblical greeting. Peace reflects a contentment with our safety, welfare, and happiness. Peace is a condition of freedom from strife, external or internal. Peace is a comprehensive gift from God representing reconciliation with him. One commentator says that peace is "fearing nothing from God and content with our earthly lot whatever sort that is."[1]

For us to have peace, soundness, wholeness, and completeness, we

---

1. Everett F. Harrison, *Baker's Dictionary of Theology* (Grand Rapids: Baker, 1960), 399.

must discover God's order. Do you accept by faith that you are right with God because of Christ's life, death, and resurrection? Do you know *(yada)* with head and heart what right act(s) God has prepared for you to do? I sometimes struggle with "right acts" or "good works" because it sounds as if I'm living under the Law, but Joshua 5 shows us a situation where "righteousness and peace kiss each other" (Psalm 85:10).

We're about to see how the breastplate of righteousness and the shoes of peace complement each other in the midst of spiritual warfare. More than any other pieces of God's armor, these two must be tightly fastened on our souls *before* we fight the good fight! While you are working through this chapter, keep these two thoughts in mind: (1) Righteousness can mean being right in character and being right with God. The former gives us present peace; the latter, eternal peace; and (2) God wants us to have peace so that we can live selflessly and consider the well-being of others.

A literal translation of Ephesians 6:15 from the Greek reads: "And have shod yourselves as to the feet in readiness of the gospel of peace." Roman soldiers wore sandals bound by thongs tied over the instep and round the ankle, and the soles were thickly studded with nails. This image doesn't remind me of peace! I don't naturally think of peace as something that moves; I imagine peace as calm, still, refined, quiet. But Paul connects *peace* and *feet*—our ready and prepared feet. Ready, eager courage that comes from the gospel fills us with the peace of God. Isaiah 52:7 says, "How beautiful…are the feet of those who bring good news, who proclaim peace, who bring glad tidings, who proclaim salvation." These are the shoes of peace.

Read Joshua 5:1-12.

FIRST LOOKS

Take a few minutes to relax and clear your mind of distractions. Pray that you would be open to the Spirit.

1. Describe the focus of this passage in one sentence.

2. List the four major events of this scene in order. Next to each event, name the initiator.

3. What does *reproach* mean? How would the Israelites remember that their reproach was rolled away (verse 9)?

✐ 4. Read Exodus 12:3,11,13,23, and 27. Define the following terms or explain their significance.

Passover

"The tenth day of this month" (Exodus 12:3)

blood

how the Israelites ate the meal

What connection do you see between the first Passover and the Passover that was celebrated in Joshua 5?

5. Who would feed the Israelites from now on?

Read Ephesians 6:14b,15.
6. What vital organ does a breastplate cover?

7. Define *righteousness* and *peace.*

8. Look back at the Joshua passage in light of these verses in Ephesians. What made the Israelites *right* in God's eyes? And what will give them a future *peace?*

CUT TO THE HEART

The Lord God of Israel initiated a covenant with the Israelites four hundred years before they crossed the Jordan River, and God does not break his covenant. The problem was that the Israelites had disobeyed God and had wandered in the desert for forty years, so the covenant was broken and God's peace *could not be enjoyed.* But in this particular window of Israel's history, the people were obedient to God and emotionally close to him (see Joshua 5:6-8). God's instructions to the Israelites show how deeply he understands human emotional and psychological makeup. God issued ordinances that would produce a future peace, a future confidence. He was planning ahead for the Israelites' well-being during times of war. He was teaching them what *his* job was—to lead and care for them—and what *their* job was—to obediently move forward with peace of mind. In the Joshua story we see that the work of righteousness would be peace, and the effect of righteousness would be "quietness and confidence forever" (Isaiah 32:17). Think of right acts as seeds and of peace as their fruit.

The Amorites and Canaanites (these names were used interchangeably) lived in the land promised to the Israelites. These people groups worshiped Baal and other pagan gods, and they were immersed in a lifestyle of materialism and sensuality. After the Israelites entered Canaan, they were continually drawn to these pagan gods, so God established the covenant of circumcision as a way of setting his chosen people apart from the godless cultures around them. Circumcision was a sign of the original covenant

God made with Abraham. The term *circumcise* literally means "to remove the foreskin of the male penis." Metaphorically, it's referred to in the book of Deuteronomy as "the circumcision of the heart." This great and universal sign represents cutting off the old life and beginning a new life with God. By circumcising our hearts before God, we find peace in the following ways:

1. *Being made right with God.* It's tempting to classify the circumcision of the Israelites as an act—a code of righteousness—that made them God's chosen people, but that interpretation would minimize God's goodness. God made a covenant with Abraham; it was his agreement, his commitment to the Israelites. No matter what they did or didn't do, they were still God's chosen people.

God commanded Joshua to circumcise the Israelite men as a sign of obedience. Circumcision was a painful process that required time for healing. One can imagine that it was a humbling experience as well. The vulnerability of the Israelite men in this scene astounds me: The enemy nations could very easily have attacked while all of Israel's fighting men were physically indisposed. Here we catch a glimpse of why this nation did not practice the covenant signs during the desert period: Disobedience to the voice of the Lord produces an anxious fear in our hearts that keeps us from being vulnerable with God and our community. We don't want to risk taking time to rest and heal because the enemy of fear keeps us walking in circles, wringing our hands.

The Israelites had to be circumcised before they could enjoy certain political and religious privileges. Passover was a privilege; circumcision was a prerequisite. Biblical writers often compare the outward act of circumcision to inward spiritual renewal (see Deuteronomy 30:6 and Jeremiah 9:25). The apostle Paul illustrated this putting off the old and putting on the new in the act of circumcision and the ordinance of baptism. This act of circumcision is meaningless, though, if our hearts are not circumcised. What does a circumcised heart have to do with the breastplate of righteousness, and what does that look like for us today?

The Greek word for breastplate is *thorax*. The function of the breastplate was to cover the vital organs of the body, particularly the heart. Paul tells us that the breastplate of *righteousness* protects our hearts. Righteousness can mean being right in character and conduct and being right with God. Just as truth has two meanings for us—who God is and who we are—so does righteousness, but for now, let's think about being right with God.

An uncircumcised heart is closed to good influences and beautiful impressions. A circumcised heart—a heart that's been cut open—is set apart from the ordinary. Baptism is one of the ways that God has ordained to set us apart to him and demonstrate that we have been made right with him. But here's a freeing thought: Baptism is more than an outward public ritual; it's an expression of the deep inner transformation that God has performed in our hearts and minds through faith. God uses baptism to peel back the foreskin of our hearts, revealing the depraved thoughts, the mental imbalances, the impulsions, obsessions, addictions, fears, insecurities, arrogance, isolation, and prejudices, and write his ways on our inward parts.

What God writes on my inward parts, my soul, may not look like what he writes on another person's soul. But what is identical is that *God* writes it. It's his doing; it gives me a new moral nature that longs to hear his voice and to please him. Once we read his writing on our minds and hearts, we experience a gladness unparalleled by any other experience! When we realize that we'll never again be able to live without his initiative, we are motivated to open our hearts to him. We need to lift our souls to God privately and pray as Henri Nouwen so succinctly prayed:

> Listen, O Lord, to my prayers. Listen to my desire to be with you,
> to dwell in your house and to let my whole being be filled with your
> presence. But none of this is possible without you. When you are
> not the one who fills me, I'm soon filled with endless thoughts and

concerns that divide me and tear me away from you. Even thoughts about you, good spiritual thoughts, can be little more than distractions when you are not their author.... Let me at least remain open to your initiative.[2]

My friend, opening your heart to God's initiative may seem weak, but you will find strength in being right with him. Opening yourself to God makes you vulnerable and means that you have to be real, but once you experience his cutting back the layers of your heart, you will know that no relationship, no book, no concept, no conference can bring you closer to God than God himself. What words has God written on your inward parts?

2. Being right in character and conduct. Righteousness can also mean being right in character and conduct. For the Israelites, circumcision was the next right act at that point in time. For us, baptism is the next right act after we receive Christ because God tells us to do it. God gave the Israelites circumcision to separate them from the pagan cultures around them; God has given us baptism to identify us with a community of believers, a royal community, a chosen people. It's the next right act that draws us closer to his holiness. God's forever commitment to us was given after Christ's life, death, and resurrection. For an Israelite, sealing God's covenant with circumcision was like a newly married husband and wife engaging in sexual intercourse: They're still married even if they don't have sex, but the act of intercourse consummates their souls and binds them together. The act of baptism binds us to God and to the community of people who are present.

After forty years of disobedience, with a sting of pain the chosen people were set apart from the heathen cultures. In response to sealing the covenant, God renamed the city Gilgal, which means "rolled away the

---

2. Henri Nouwen, *A Cry for Mercy* (New York: Doubleday, 1981), 13.

reproach" (Joshua 5:9), and he received the praises of his people at a Passover celebration the next day.

So there were the Israelites on the other side of the Jordan, no longer in slavery, no longer dependent upon manna, no longer wondering about God's will for their lives. They had reached the Promised Land, and this most amazing truth was birthed: God can teach his people through ordinary means. When the Israelites celebrated Passover this time, they ate food from the land rather than eating manna from heaven. A source of strength not known before circumcision was now emerging: This new strength was peace—embedded in their memories, their souls, their spirits. The shoes of peace were on their feet, and the breastplate of righteousness was fastened securely just in time for the battle of Jericho. Before we look at this battle in the next chapter, let's delve a little deeper into the Joshua story to see *how God's shoes of peace prepare us for the battles ahead.*

Read Joshua 5:13-15.

TAKING IT IN

9. Briefly write how the following events or places separated the Hebrew people from the surrounding cultures:

circumcision

Gilgal

Passover

the appearance of the commander of the Lord's army

10. Why do you think this scene between Joshua and the commander of the Lord's army did not take place immediately after the crossing? What do you think God's purposes were for this order of doing things?

Imagine a militarily clad Joshua down on his face in reverence. Picture his shoes beside him and his sword on the ground. Imagine another military man (probably much larger) standing over him with a drawn sword and a holy light around him. With this scene in mind, answer the following questions.

11. If the shoes of peace represent a readiness or preparedness, what significance do you see in God's telling Joshua to remove his shoes? (You might also look at Exodus 3:2-5.)

12. In the Joshua story, how has God's breastplate of righteousness protected the hearts of Joshua and the Israelites? What will give them peace when they go to war?

13. Explain how peace gave Joshua the strength to say, "What message does my Lord have for his servant?" (Joshua 5:14).

READY TO MOVE WITH BEAUTIFUL FEET

In Joshua 5, the Israelites were prepared, ready, and eager to do the next right thing—that's a sign of strong souls. Somehow they intuitively knew that the peace, the well-being God had given them was not just for the present. I must confess to you that immediately following my times alone with God, after he has filled me with himself and I have that sense of well-being, my first thoughts are not always about what he wants me to do next! When I'm experiencing that kind of peace, I want to keep the treasure for myself and bury it. What do you usually do when you have a sense of well-being?

Celebrating Passover and eating the produce of the land is a sign, just like circumcision, of a holy people responding to their covenant relationship with God. What does that look like for us as a Christian community in the twenty-first century? God ordained baptism and Communion and the church; now it's our turn to respond to each of his ordinances. This is the next right thing for us to do, just as circumcision and Passover were the next right things for the Israelites to do. The *shoes of peace* imply a readiness, which implies an eagerness. If we are not eager about church,

Communion, and baptism, they become only empty external rituals to us. If we do not do the next right thing—if we get stalled as individuals or communities—we have conflict in our souls.

There isn't a formula for obedience to God. Certainly, we accomplish tasks to have peace, and we retreat from ordinary life to have peace. But a life of continual contemplation doesn't always mean we are listening to God. To understand where peace comes from and how it gives us strength, we cannot embrace ordinary human reasoning. We need a holy logic. As physicist Neils Bohr said, "The opposite of a true statement is a false statement, but the opposite of a profound truth can be another profound truth."[3] *Peace occurs when we respond eagerly to God's initiatives and do the next right thing.* For the Israelites, circumcision, Passover, the last of the manna, and the appearance of a captain were important, but the order of events and who was initiating them were even more important—it's a holy logic. In other words, you may have everything you need in life, but what is important is what God wants for your life. What are the next right things for us collectively as God's chosen people?

If we accept the provisions of baptism, church, and Communion as part of God's covenant love for us, we'll have peace. If we refuse baptism, if we take Communion unprepared, if we critically or casually attend church, we assert our individualism and refuse to yield to our collective responsibility as God's holy people. Are we uncomfortable being baptized today? Do we devoutly prepare our hearts for Communion? Perhaps these sorts of public displays of commitment to God are so unusual in today's culture that it's embarrassing for us to be set apart from the crowd in such an antiquated way. Or maybe we *want* to be set apart at times for the sake of appearances. What is most important is what God has written on our hearts. If we are eager for relationship with him, we will do what he wants

---

3. Neils Bohr, quoted in Parker Palmer, *The Active Life: A Spirituality of Work, Creativity, and Caring* (Hoboken, N.J.: John Wiley & Sons, 1999), 15.

us to do next. This may mean expressing our relationship with him in a public way, even if it makes us uncomfortable, or it may mean stepping back from a leadership role because he wants us to be closer to him individually before we step out in public. The most important thing is for our hearts, our inward parts, our souls to have God's holy writing on them. This is what brings us strength and peace.

As we think about what it means to be peaceful, it's important to be very honest about peace of mind in the midst of tragedy or great loss. God has allowed me to experience personal loss, but even more profound have been the losses of the people closest to me. I've held friends' shaking bodies as they've grieved, and I've heard them crying out to God in the dark nights of their souls. I cannot say that these precious souls have a sense of well-being at those times, but I will say this: God doesn't *give* them his peace; God himself *is* their peace. It's not that the armor of God is not powerful when great tragedy comes, but sometimes the next right thing to do in the midst of tragedy is to fall to the floor in a heap and let God come closer to you than ever before.

LIVING OUT THE NEXT THING

In the last three years, I've discovered the real reasons I go to church. These reasons became obvious when our family was churchless. After we moved out west, we church-hopped for more than two years and were sobered by the feeling that we didn't belong. I began to dread Sundays, knowing I would worship the living God with a group of unknown people as if I were watching a movie; my presence really didn't count. I knew that God's presence mattered far more than mine did, but the emptiness was very real.

Toward the end of our search, Brad and I prayed in earnest for God's leading. We asked him what was wrong with us that we could not have peace about one single church. Then we realized we were asking the wrong questions. We'd been so concerned with finding a church that did things "right" that we were missing the real reasons for attending church. We needed to focus not on our own "needs," but on where God was calling us.

The day we stepped into the little white church on the hill fifteen miles from our home, our hearts and minds knew they had found a home to worship God. We would not have chosen a church with fewer than one hundred people ("that's too intimate"), but God wanted us to know the eagerness of these few people each Sunday morning. We would not have chosen a congregation that sings songs with only a piano for accompaniment, but God wanted us to worship him away from the polished music so he could fill us with his Spirit. We would not have chosen a church that didn't offer an upscale children's program, but God wanted our family to sit together during worship.

When Brad and I tried to follow our own order of how we thought things should be, we didn't have peace. When we realized and accepted that God has an order that may be different from ours, we were able to receive his peace. I've discovered that God's order for my spiritual life brings out the best in me and shows me his character more clearly. His provisions of baptism, Communion, and community are good; they are the next right thing for me to do. It's like a circle—people are baptized regularly, we attend church weekly, we take Communion monthly—and this circle of doing, this circle of discipline, brings a peace to my heart and mind. If we take the Joshua story seriously, we realize that the peace God gave the Israelites was for a future purpose: He wanted them to remember this peace of mind when they were fighting battles.

God in his Sovereignty had work for the Israelites to do. To be specific, he had a battle for them to fight. God has work for you and me to do as well; he has battles for us to fight, and he wants us to be prepared with the peace he has given us. Before you and I can fight any battle with the power of God, we must have an encounter, or many encounters, with his holiness. Like Joshua, we need to remove our shoes to get prepared! To wear the shoes of peace, to put on the breastplate of righteousness, to know the strength of soul that we long to know, we must, without mincing our words, fall facedown in reverence and ask, "What message does my Lord have for his servant?" (Joshua 5:15).

MAKING IT REAL

I think you will enjoy reading Sarah Orne Jewett, a wonderfully descriptive and gentle writer. In this scene the narrator realizes the conflict in her soul as she goes about her day but longs to be somewhere else.

A DUNNET SHEPHERDESS BY SARAH ORNE JEWETT[4]

It was only twenty minutes past six on a summer morning, but we both sat down to rest as if the activities of the day were over. Mrs. Todd rocked gently for a time, and seemed to be lost, though not poorly, like Macbeth, in her thoughts. At last she resumed relations with her actual surroundings. "I shall now put my lobsters on. They'll make us a good supper," she announced. "Then I can let the fire out for all day; give it a holiday, same's William. You can have a little one now, nice an' hot, if you ain't got all the breakfast you want. Yes, I'll put the lobsters on. William was very thoughtful to bring 'em over; William *is* thoughtful; if he only had a spark o' ambition, there be few could match him."

This unusual concession was afforded a sympathetic listener from the depths of the kitchen closet. Mrs. Todd was getting out her old iron lobster pot, and began to speak of prosaic affairs. I hoped that I should hear something more about her brother and their island life, and sat idly by the kitchen

---

4. Sarah Orne Jewett, *A Dunnet Shepherdess* (Boston: Houghton Mifflin, 1896; reprint New York: Dover, 1994), 137-9.

window looking at the morning glories that shaded it, believing that some flaw of wind might set Mrs. Todd's mind on its former course. Then it occurred to me that she had spoken about our supper rather than our dinner, and I guessed that she might have some great scheme before her for the day.

When I had loitered for some time and there was no further word about William, and at last I was conscious of receiving no attention whatever, I went away. It was something of a disappointment to find that she put no hindrance in the way of my usual morning affairs, of going up to the empty little white schoolhouse on the hill where I did my task of writing. I had been almost sure of a holiday when I discovered that Mrs. Todd was likely to take one herself; we had not been far afield to gather herbs and pleasures for many days now, but a little later she had silently vanished. I found my luncheon ready on the table in the little entry, wrapped in its shining old homespun napkin, and as if by way of special consolation, there was a stone bottle of Mrs. Todd's best spruce beer, with a long piece of cod line wound round it by which it could be lowered for coolness into the deep schoolhouse well.

I walked away with a dull supply of writing-paper and these provisions, feeling like a reluctant child who hopes to be called back at every step. There was no relenting voice to be heard, and when I reached the schoolhouse, I found that I had left an open window and a swinging shutter the day before, and the sea wind that blew at evening had fluttered my poor sheaf of papers all about the room.

So the day did not begin very well, and I began to recognize that it was one of the days when nothing could be done without company. The truth was that my heart had gone trouting with William, but it would have been too selfish to say a word even to one's self about spoiling his day. If there is one way above another of getting so close to nature that one simply is a piece of nature, following a primeval instinct with perfect self-forgetfulness and for-getting everything except the dreamy consciousness of pleasant freedom, it is to take the course of a shady trout brook. The dark pools and the sunny shallows beckon one on; the wedge of sky between the trees on either bank, the speaking, companioning noise of the water, the amazing importance of what one is doing, and the constant sense of life and beauty make a strange transformation of the quick hours. I had a sudden memory of all this, and another, and another. I could not get myself free from "fishing and wishing."

At that moment I heard the unusual sound of wheels, and I looked past the high-growing thicket of wild-roses and straggling sumach to see the white nose and meagre shape of the Caplin horse; then I saw William sitting in the open wagon, with a small expectant smile upon his face.

"I've got two lines," he said. "I was quite a piece up the road. I thought perhaps 'twas so you'd feel like going."

There was enough excitement for most occasions in hearing William speak three sentences at once. Words seemed but vain to me at that bright moment. I stepped back from the schoolhouse window with a beating heart. The spruce-beer bottle was not yet in the well, and with that and my luncheon, and Pleasure at the helm, I went out into the happy world. The land breeze was blowing, and, as we turned away, I saw a flutter of white go past the window as I left the schoolhouse and my morning's work to their neglected fate.

14. What has brought a "constant sense of life and beauty" to your soul this past month?

15. In *A Dunnet Shepherdess*, the author's statement "I began to recognize that it was one of the days when nothing could be done without company" suggests a purpose for community. How is

the author's need to be with people similar to the purposes of community described in Joshua 5 (i.e., eating together, worshiping together, etc.)?

16. Reread the quote by Thomas Kelly at the beginning of the chapter. Do you feel that your external "good works"—what you do on one level—are not in harmony with your deeper self? Explain.

SIX

Dancing Our Wills to the Rhythm of God's Word

Wielding the Sword of the Spirit

Joshua 5:13-15; 6:1-19; Ephesians 6:17-18;
Revelation 1:12-18

*The voice of God does not merely approve or disapprove; it
encourages, reassures, informs and instructs.*

—Selwyn Hughes, *Every Day with Jesus*

During the course of writing this study, I spent time at the Trappist Abbey, a Benedictine monastery a few miles from our home. I expected days of silence and isolation in the lodge so I could write and pray. I did not, however, anticipate sitting in total silence at a dining room table with six other people. Those who know me know that this seemed an impossible task! The awkwardness increased when, by accident, we made eye contact or I could sense that someone needed the pepper. Resolving to not respond took all my energy, but the sign above the counter read "Silent Meal," so I willed myself to not make a sound—even though I was bursting with the need to ask each person several hundred questions! It actually took more focus to be silent than it would have taken to speak. Silence became an *action* for me at that table, not a passive response.

Prayer often involves the kind of active silence I experienced at the monastery. It takes intention and will to remain attentive as we listen for God. As we'll see in the story of Jericho, God is ready to speak in our silences if we are ready to hear him. How strong are we at keeping silent until God gives us a word?

BREAKING GROUND

Describe a recent time of waiting in silence for God to speak to you.

WAITING TO HEAR

I believe waiting for God to give his word is a lost art in today's Christian culture. We often expect God's answer or voice to come all at once, so we lose heart when we don't hear his response as quickly as we thought we would. The story of the fall of Jericho provides a poignant example of how listening for God's word is not something to approach casually. His voice speaks to us like a song as we journey through enemy territory. Like the Israelites, we have to remain attentive to hear his instruction—his song—and trust that his words have the power to bring down walls.

Read Joshua 5:13-15 again and 6:1-19.

FIRST LOOKS

⚲ 1. What choices did Joshua make when he realized that the commander of the Lord's army was speaking to him (5:13-15)?

2. What words in the first two verses of Joshua 6 indicate that the Israelites had entered enemy territory? How would you summarize the military plan for taking Jericho?

3. How many days did the people—including Joshua and the priests—march around the city before they spoke?

4. Reread Joshua 6:1-16 slowly and note below what the people heard for seven days.

Read Ephesians 6:17-18 and Revelation 1:12-18.

⚲ 5. How can a mouth be like a sword?

6. List several adjectives that describe God's Word or his words.

The Power of the Sword

Some scholars believe that the commander of the Lord's army in Joshua 5:13 was Christ and that the sword he wielded represented the words of God. (Such an encounter is called a *theophany,* a *Christophany,* or a manifestation of God.) In this scene Joshua was commissioned to take Jericho by the words of God—his *living and active* Word. Just as Christ (the theophany) gripped the sword with his hand, so would Joshua have to hold on to the spoken words of God. Only by embracing God's words would he survive in enemy territory.

It's helpful to look at the Ephesians text in the context of this passage in Joshua. Every piece of armor Paul referred to in Ephesians 6 is *defensive* except for the sword of the Spirit, "which is the Word of God" (verse 17). There are two Greek words for "word." One is *logos,* which is Jesus Christ (John 1:1), and the second is *rhēma,* the sayings of God that Paul referred to in Ephesians 6:17. We can't hear the sayings of God if we don't have our defensive armor on: faith, hope, peace, truth, and righteousness. But when we are prepared to defend ourselves, we are also ready to go on the offensive and fight—and God calls us to fight with the living and active sword of the Spirit. For God's Word "is sharp as a surgeon's scalpel, cutting through everything, whether doubt or defense, laying us open to listen and obey" (Hebrews 4:12, MSG).

The "sword of the Spirit" in Ephesians 6 is not referring to the Scriptures alone. The "word of God" that Paul referred to is the word spoken to us by the Holy Spirit. When we pray, we are waiting to hear the word of God with the ears of our heart so we can take his Word and fight with that powerful sword.

The Israelites provide us with a beautiful example of waiting in expectation of hearing God's word. First, they listened to instruction without question. The captain of the Lord's army provided Joshua with a detailed plan about how to operate in enemy territory: No military powers were to be used, no weapons of mass destruction. The army was not even supposed to scale the thirty-foot walls. Instead, the Israelites were instructed to carry the ark of the Lord around the city once a day for six days and seven times on the seventh day.

As the narrative progresses, we read details that we didn't see in the Lord's first directions to Joshua: The priests blew the trumpets of rams' horns. Seven priests went immediately before the ark, sounding trumpets to remind them of God's presence, and the 2.5 million people followed the ark. But the writer of this narrative waited until later to give the real clincher: The people were to be absolutely silent as they marched around the city!

Could this be an example of how God imparts his living and active word to us? Consider what was happening all around the Hebrew people. The ark was central and significant, but it wasn't God himself; it only represented him. The armed Israelite soldiers looked fierce, but they were only a symbol of intimidation. The remaining multitudes of people formed the rear guard, but they had not been trained in battle. During the march the priests were to keep sounding the trumpets (Joshua 6:13), but that was not God's final word. For God to place the enemy territory of Jericho in their hands, Joshua and the people were to *exalt the word of God above all else* by keeping silent until he spoke. Neither the ark, the priests, the trumpets, the military men, nor the multitudes had the power that one of God's words held.

Imagine this ridiculous scene and how foolish the Israelites appeared to the people of Jericho. The story gradually picks up speed and intensity. Day after day the ark, the priests, the armed soldiers, and the multitudes marched around the city walls, knowing exactly what God had said to Joshua days earlier: "I have given Jericho into your hand" (6:2, NASB). Did you hear that? That's the song of promise Joshua heard, and it's on that promise that he based his resolve. Then, suddenly, it happened—Joshua told the people to give a great shout! And with that shout of faith, the city wall fell down flat. This is the shout of faith God calls us to give when we need to intimidate the enemy or encourage a friend. Only by listening to God's instructions were the Israelites ready to respond when he spoke again.

The Israelites kept their focus. You might say they "danced their wills" to endure the wait for God's word, and it was in the waiting, in the understanding, even in the appreciating of God's instructions that they fulfilled God's will. It was God's word that brought the walls down in enemy territory. And here's where we learn how to fight with the sword of the Spirit: by waiting in prayer, by willing ourselves to wait in silence for the word of the Lord.

Similar to Joshua 3, Joshua 6 has an interesting repetition of words. The instructions to the Israelites are played over and over like the beat of a drum. Can you see how this interplay of words influenced the Israelites' resolve to keep moving? God was handing the city over to the Israelites, but many words and actions were taking place around this central act. First, the commander of the Lord's army told Joshua that the city of Jericho was a gift—signed, sealed, and delivered. Joshua repeated this promise to the people, and they responded to the rhythm of God's—and Joshua's—words to them: They danced to God's instructions. They danced their wills to the song of God's promise.

As Joshua and the people approached, partnered, and danced with their wills to the music of God's word, they *wielded the sword of the Spirit without losing their focus,* even though they looked foolish! They maintained this focus by an act of their wills. But their wills were responding to the music of God's word. This active and alive focus moved the multitudes around the walls of Jericho and brought the walls down. God's voice is the music; dancing our wills to that music is our response!

TAKING IT IN

But how do we fight with the sword of the Spirit? How do we maintain our focus and wait on God to speak? Taking time to listen in silence is an art that must be developed. Men and women throughout history who have learned to distinguish between their own imaginations and the voice of the Lord admit that it takes practice. One approach that can help us cultivate the art of listening to God is *lectio divina* (divine reading). Lectio divina is an exercise in slow, contemplative praying of Scripture. In a group it is often done aloud. But whether we are reading silently or aloud, lectio divina means not just reading the Word, but listening to it, "turning our eyes into ears," as the classical writers observed.

One of my favorite ways to experience lectio divina is to slowly read two or more passages of Scripture in succession in order to learn more about God through the continuity of his Word.

In the following exercise, I'm going to ask you to read through Joshua 6 with Psalm 29 as the backdrop. You may want to read just one or two sets of these scriptures right now and do the others at another time. If you are in a group, you may want to read one set now and do the others individually throughout the week.

As you read, you may sense the Holy Spirit revealing something to your spirit. If you do, write down the verse or phrase that spoke to you. Ask the Holy Spirit to teach you something new about God through this verse or phrase. I'm praying that the awe and wonder of God's words in our world and in your personal life will move you to a deeper understanding of how to listen to his voice.

Listening for the Gentle Touch of Christ in the Word

7. Read aloud the first two passages listed below. (If you are in a group, have one person read and the others listen attentively for a part of the reading that may be especially meaningful to them. Throughout this exercise, a group leader should coordinate the process and facilitate sharing.)

   • Read Psalm 29:1-2 and Joshua 6:1-5.
   • Read Psalm 29:3-4 and Joshua 6:6-10.
   • Read Psalm 29:5-7 and Joshua 6:11-17.
   • Read Psalm 29:8-9 and Joshua 6:18-23.
   • Read Psalm 29:10-11 and Joshua 6:24-27.

8. Be silent for one or two minutes. Silently repeat the word or phrase that caught your spirit's attention.

9. If you are in a group, allow time for each person to share aloud a word or phrase that was particularly meaningful to him or her. If you are doing this study alone, write down that word or phrase. One or two words is enough for now.

How Christ the Word Speaks to Me

10. Read the same set of scriptures again. If you are in a group, have a different person read this time.

11. Be silent for two or three minutes. Reflect on the question, Where does the content of this reading touch my life today?

12. Briefly share aloud your response to the preceding question ("I see…"; "I hear…"). If you are doing this study alone, write down your response.

What Christ the Word Invites Me to Do

13. Read the same set of scriptures a third time.
14. Be silent for two or three minutes. Reflect on how you would complete this statement: "I believe that today or this week God wants me to…"

15. How did reading the psalm along with each part of the Jericho story change your thinking about the power of God's voice? You may want to take time this week to journal your response. Write until you have a sense of completion.

16. After doing this exercise, what new insights do you have about the effect marching around the city walls thirteen times had on the Hebrew people? What effect do you think it would have

had on you? Why do you think God asked the Israelites to march as they did?

In Enemy Territory

We have to remain focused to hear the word of God, and when we do hear his word, we are to wield our swords with an iron will and continue to listen for instructions. When we receive instructions, we must stay focused no matter what the cost. It's a choice, but it's a choice toward soul strength.

We don't just read a passage of Scripture one time and decide we have an answer or instructions from God. As odd as the Hebrew people looked that week marching around those brown, rocky city walls, they still waited for the final word. That's how Christians who yearn for soul strength should respond: We will ourselves to read Scripture, apply it to our circumstances, pray consistently, and keep on marching while we wait. While we are silent we are still interacting with God and people—we are cleaning the house, writing letters, helping our neighbors, worshiping God. God promises to lead us, and he has good things to give us. What is he giving you? Have you waited patiently for a word from God and listened until he's given you the command to shout?

The power of God's word in "enemy territory" became very real to me about three years ago during an extremely intense time in my married life. Brad and I had just moved our family cross-country and found ourselves suffering the pains and blows of spiritual warfare. What made these attacks so unexpected was all the time, prayers, support, direction, and planning that had gone into following "God's will" for our work and ministry. Feeling confident that all signs led to moving from an East Coast college to a West Coast university, we willingly packed our bags. Our family and friends shared in this confidence, helped us pack, showered us with a grand going-away gala, and drove us to the airport, saying all the while: "This truly is God's will for your family." Every one of us firmly believed that.

When the attacks came with a vengeance, we immediately started questioning if we had "misheard" God's voice. On one particular night both Brad and I confessed to each other that we thought we might be losing our minds. Our external circumstances appeared "normal," but internally we were struggling with darkness. The Enemy knew where we were so very weak. He knew that most of our confidence rested in things going right, in others' opinions, and in decisive attitudes.

I studied the Bible and prayed regularly, but I was not prepared for the way these attacks exposed my true weaknesses. Imagine yourself sprawled out on the ground with a strong hand around your neck and a voice telling you to give up. That's the place I found myself. I loved my family too much to let everything go, so I resolved to fight back. I realized that I could not move through a day unless my will chose to hear and act on the voice of the Lord.

Through that experience I entered the kingdom of broken souls, those souls who readily admit that we are defeated if we aren't actively engaged with God and his Word. Once I entered the Enemy's territory, God's will and his Word became a vivid reality in my moments—not just during my days or weeks. Being willing to hear his word and do it sustains me now. When I don't wait for his word, I give the Enemy a chance to destroy the soundness of my mind. A part of me is embarrassed to admit this weakness, but it's in this weakness that I've discovered authentic soul strength.

MAKING IT REAL

Jonathan Edwards is considered one of America's greatest theologians. He spent his life writing about the importance of religious "affections" or the passions that move the will to act. This is a small selection from his writings:

RELIGIOUS AFFECTIONS BY JONATHAN EDWARDS[1]

That religion which God requires, and will accept, does not consist in weak, dull, and lifeless wishes, raising us but a little above a state of indifference: God, in his word, greatly insists upon it, that we be good in earnest, "fervent in spirit," and our hearts vigorously engaged in religion....

If we be not in good earnest in religion, and our wills and inclinations be not strongly exercised, we are nothing. The things of religion are so great, that there can be no suitableness in the exercises of our hearts, to their nature and importance, unless they be lively and powerful. In nothing is vigor in the actings of our inclinations so requisite, as in relation; and in nothing is lukewarmness so odious. True religion is evermore a powerful thing; and the power of it appears, in the first place in the inward exercises of it in the heart, where is the principal and original seat of it....

The Author of the human nature has not only given affections to men, but has made them very much the spring of men's actions.... And as in worldly things, worldly affections are very much the spring of men's motion and action; so in religious matters, the spring of their actions is very religious affection: he that has doctrinal knowledge and speculation only, without affection, never is engaged in the business of religion.

17. Why do you think our emotions or affections matter when it comes to doctrine and theology?

---

1. Jonathan Edwards, *The Religious Affections* in *The Works of Jonathan Edwards,* vol. 1 (Edinburgh: Banner of Truth, 1974), 237.

18. What, if anything, did the Holy Spirit bring to your attention as you read this text?

19. Consider Edward's words:

> That religion which God requires…does not consist in weak, dull, and lifeless wishes, raising us but a little above a state of indifference: God, in his word, greatly insists…that we be…"fervent in spirit," and our hearts vigorously engaged in religion.…

What impact do our religious affections have on our ability to hear the words of God? to "dance our wills" to the rhythm of those words?

20. Observe your heart, your will, your passions this week and note what motivates them to action.

SEVEN

GUARDING AGAINST SELFISH DESIRES

Receiving the Helmet of Hope and Salvation

JOSHUA 6:18,22-23; 7; EPHESIANS 6:17;
ISAIAH 59:17; 1 THESSALONIANS 5:8

Worship is the submission of all our nature to God. It is the quickening of conscience by His holiness; the nourishment of mind with His truth; the purifying of imagination by His beauty; the opening of the heart to His love; the surrender of will to His purpose—and all this is gathered up in adoration, the most selfless emotion of which our nature is capable and therefore the chief remedy for that self-centredness which is our original sin and the source of actual sin.

—WILLIAM TEMPLE, *Readings in St. John's Gospel*

In Bible times expensive materials such as linen and silk were used for clothing. Even poor people wore clothes made from linen, but the wealthy used a fine-combed linen. Both men and women dressed in outer as well as inner garments (a woman's outer garment flowed to the floor over her feet), and both men and women decorated their outer garments with jewels depending on their financial resources and social status.

A beautiful outer garment was a sign of the highest prestige—the differences between common people, common priests, and the high priests were noticeable. The high priests wore beautifully decorated breastplates (with different stones for each tribe), and much time and preparation were spent on their outer garments.

Such rich clothing was coveted. People particularly desired Babylonian garments because, at the time, Babylon was one of the greatest cities in the world—the leader in culture, the arts, and education. Anything from Babylon was considered to be the best. Even though the Babylonian Empire had weakened by the time the Jewish people entered the Promised Land, it was still highly exalted in everyone's thoughts and minds.

In Joshua 7, we find out that someone in the Israelite tribe had sinned; he had taken for himself Babylonian money and a beautiful Babylonian garment, "a mantle from Shinar" (verse 21, NASB). As the Israelite community learned, when we do not guard our minds from coveting what is not ours, we fail to place our hope in what God offers. But when we highly exalt God in our minds, we desire the hope he has for us. Receiving the helmet of hope and salvation is essential to clothing our souls in strength.

BREAKING GROUND

What is your "mantle from Shinar"? As you go through your day, what do you really *hope* for? What do you want?

The Power of Selfish Desire

Community is an important theme in Joshua and Ephesians. A number of the images and descriptions Paul used in Ephesians make it clear that the church at Ephesus belonged to a larger group of Christians. In his desire for the Ephesians to understand their identity within the universal church, Paul encouraged these Christians to grasp with greater awareness the blessings and privileges that come with this identity (see Ephesians 1:3-14). Here's our connection with the Joshua story: The last verse of Joshua 6 says that "the LORD was with Joshua, and his fame spread throughout the land." The first verse of Joshua 7 says, "But the Israelites acted unfaithfully." What we are about to see is how one individual brought about God's judgment on the entire Israelite community because he "[ran] after other gods" (Psalm 16:4) and failed to *receive* what God wanted to give him.

Read Joshua 6:18,22-23 and Joshua 7.

First Looks

1. Compare Rahab's rescue with Joshua 7:1. Why was Rahab's family spared? Why were the Israelites considered "unfaithful"?

2. In one sentence, summarize Joshua 7:1-13.

3. If Joshua 6 was all about victory, what would you say chapter 7 was all about?

Read Ephesians 6:17; Isaiah 59:17; and 1 Thessalonians 5:8.
4. Why do you think that the hope of salvation is used as a helmet?

5. What do you think are the key differences between eternal salvation and immediate salvation?

RESCUED FROM THE DEFEAT OF SELFISHNESS

Let's look carefully at the sequence that leads from (1) a community receiving God's blessing to (2) a community living in defeat to (3) a community being rescued!

1. Receiving God's abundant blessing. Just moments before the battle at Ai, Joshua and the Israelites were basking in the awesome presence and power of God. They were blessed with everything! How could Joshua and his men have missed the mark so profoundly that thirty-six men were killed and the Israelites were defeated? The mental confusion over this defeat must have been torture. We can understand Joshua's expression of grief to God, but what happened?

2. The defeat that comes with sin. Here we see the consequences when one person decides that taking from God is more satisfying than receiving from him. In Joshua 6, God commanded Joshua and the Israelites to gather all the treasure, money, and valuable goods from the spoils of Jericho for use in the service of the tabernacle (verse 19). Jericho was the first-fruits of God (Exodus 23:19), and everything in it belonged to him. The Israelites had been told that keeping any of the gold or treasure would bring a curse: God would not be with them, and his blessings would stop. Even after the city was completely destroyed, the Israelites were cautioned to keep their desires in check and not take any of the gold and treasures for themselves because those "devoted things" did not belong to them.

Joshua knew the Amorites were a sinful people. If Israel were destroyed in battle, who would represent God's great name? Joshua's chief concern was God's reputation, and yet it was because of Joshua's confidence, his newly acquired fame, his I-already-know-how-this-works mindset that he took matters into his own hands and failed to first receive instructions from God. So confident was he in his ability to fight for God's great name that Joshua was flabbergasted that God allowed the Israelites to be defeated!

3. Waiting to be rescued from selfishness and grief. Joshua responded to what he considered an act of injustice with a swift and reverent act of grief. He went up to the ark that represented the presence of God, tore his outer garment (an act that was the custom of his day), and called on the name of God using two Hebrew names: *Donay Yhwh.* We can almost hear his moaning, "Ah, Sovereign LORD." Then he boldly questioned the Almighty.

God responded to Joshua boldly, quickly, and honestly, like a king who is tired of repeating himself: There is sin in the community of the Israelites. The consequences of that sin are grave: "*I will not be with you anymore* unless you destroy whatever among you is devoted to destruction" (Joshua 7:12, emphasis added).

The story of Achan illustrates both a pattern and a principle that are extremely relevant to Christians today: First, God showered his people with blessings, then the people sinned, and judgment followed. When the people repented and returned to God, he rescued them, and the blessing returned.

This is also the pattern for us as individuals. On my journey toward soul strength, God brought me to a place where I was willing for him to search my heart and know my mind. And in the process, he allowed me to see what was offensive to him. It was humbling and painful to see what I was really like, to see the thoughts I really had. This was not easy, but, my friend, I can stand again, and I promise you this: The rewards of this journey toward God far outweigh the pain. I encourage you to enter into the vulnerability of wearing the armor of God because only then will you find true strength!

Read Joshua 6:18 and 7:6-12,21 again.

Taking It In

6. Read Psalm 121:3-8. The words "watches over" have the same meaning as the Hebrew words "keep away" in Joshua 6:18. Write down what you think it means that God "watches over" you.

7. How could the Israelites "keep away" from or "watch over" the beautiful things sitting right in front of their faces?

8. As you read Achan's admission of coveting, in what way do you think he failed to guard or keep watch over his heart and mind? Do you think his desire was sinful? Why or why not?

9. What do Joshua's and the elders' positions before the ark of the Lord tell us about their attitudes? (Compare Joshua 7:6 with Joshua 5:14.)

10. Compare and contrast Joshua's complaints and God's concerns.

11. Before God told Joshua what was going on, what did he demand of Joshua (7:10)? Why do you think he wanted Joshua to take this position?

RECEIVING HOPE

God created the soul's capacity to long, to hope, to expect. The word *covet* is partially defined as "to delight in." I'm convinced that God wants our souls to experience delight, and I agree with the many writers who say that our desires are not strong enough, that we are too easily pleased. Recently my husband and I have seen the need to teach our daughters the meaning of contentment—"being happy with what you have." But we emphasize the *happy* part; we don't want them to just settle for what they have, but to squeal with delight with what they have and what they will have in the future!

In Greek and Roman times, *hope* (*elpis* in the Greek) had a neutral meaning of "the expectation of good or evil." Some Greek philosophers treated hope cynically, and others lifted it high. In 1 Thessalonians 5:8, hope means "to desire something with confident expectation of its fulfillment." Hope begins in the mind. We can hope for the things God has for us, or we can hope for the things that belong to other people or to God. Colossians 1 states that everything was made for God (see verse 16). That means everything we have and own are gifts to us from God.

Just as Joshua cried out, "Ah, Sovereign Lord," we often groan in our spirits when Christ in us recognizes our sin—recognizes that we have hoped in something other than God. We feel emotionally and mentally lost. But it's in the expression of our grief for ourselves and others that we receive, even welcome, God's gift of salvation to us. How does this work?

When we receive the helmet of true hope and place it upon our minds, we have the ability to look and feel beyond our present grief, desires, and wishes. Joshua fell facedown onto the ground because he had no hope in his current circumstances. Look at what he said to God: "Why did you move us…to kill us? If only we hadn't followed you!" (Joshua 7:7, author's paraphrase). I so appreciate Joshua's honesty and passion in his relationship with God. How often are you and I completely honest with God about our feelings of hopelessness? Do we ever fall facedown onto the ground? Joshua and the elders put dust on their heads, symbolizing from whence they came. An honest cry to God during our most grievous moments is an act of worship. Hiding sin leaves us hopeless. Achan tried to hide his sin, but Joshua confronted sin, telling Achan to "give glory to the LORD" and "give him praise" (Joshua 7:19).

What happened next illustrates how we receive the helmet of hope and how we put it on our minds. For the first time in the story, we see Joshua's weakness: He was ignorant of his people's sin. In response to this weakness, God told Joshua to "stand up" and asked him, "What are you doing down on your face?" (Joshua 7:10). God did not review why he had brought the Israelites across the Jordan nor did he defend his great name. He played it straight: Israel had sinned. That knowledge invited Joshua and the Israelites to wear the helmet of hope because it opened their eyes to their need for *God's* salvation. Can't you just see Joshua's eyes opening wide and hear him saying, "Oh! So that's what's going on!"

Joshua's response is vital for us. Once God has revealed our sin to us individually and corporately, we must stand up; we must come back to life. Do you struggle with staying in places of hopelessness because of your sin or grief? I know I do. I am learning to guard my mind against dwelling too much on pity for myself or others.

We also receive the helmet of hope and salvation when we destroy whatever we have taken that is not ours. Then we wait for God to give us what is truly ours. Picture whatever you exalt as your helmet, and imagine yourself in battle with that helmet on your head. If you covet a sexual relationship that is not yours, sex is always on your mind, and when the opportunity presents itself, you will act out what you're obsessing about. Or maybe you want so much for your children to be admired that their success is always on your mind and you consistently "steal" another child's spotlight with your words of comparison.

The Greek word *dechomai,* which means "to receive," is used in Ephesians 6:17 to express the idea that we *receive* hope, and once we receive it, our minds are protected in battle, just as a warrior's head was protected by a brass helmet. Do you see the imagery here? When you and I satisfy our longings with other people's things, we violate God's promise to provide for all our needs. When we see something we want, our minds drive us to it, and that thing becomes our hope. Figuratively, we hope this thing will "save" us from being average. Our competitive natures want to be the best. On the other hand, when *God's salvation,* God's rescuing us, becomes our hope, our minds are secure, safe, guarded, watched over.

Achan could have had everything he wanted if he had only waited (see Joshua 8:1-2). Deuteronomy 19:14 hit me hard one night after I asked God for something that did not belong to me. I read these words as their truth stung me: "Do not move your neighbor's boundary stone set up by your predecessors in the inheritance you receive in the land the LORD your God is giving you to possess." Whenever covetous thoughts come—and let me tell you, they come when my guard is down—I start praying as honestly as I can to God. I admit my desire to move my neighbor's boundary stone, I confess how it would make me feel better about myself if I had what they had, and then somehow I start asking God to help me want what I already have. I list in my mind what God has given me to possess, and I pray for even more passion in taking possession of what I already own. The helmet of hope guards us from coveting what others have and what we think we deserve. On this side of the Cross, our living hope is that Jesus Christ is alive and, like Joshua, pleading with God on our behalf. I am struck by the meaning of Joshua's name: "Jehovah saves."

Why do we trick ourselves into thinking that God does not know what secrets we hold deep within our hearts? God is omniscient; he is there with us; he knows our hearts. The tenth commandment sums up the other nine: You shall not covet your neighbor's...anything! Why do you and I want to highly exalt what someone else has? Or exalt what we think we deserve? The Creator of our souls knows our passions for possessions are strong; he just wants those passions to be for him so that he can give to us more abundantly.

MAKING IT REAL

At first read, these sentences from Shakespeare's *King Richard II* appear to be spoken by a humble king. However, in this scene King Richard did not want to fight for his kingship and preferred dethronement. Instead, he wanted to think about the things mentioned in this reading rather than about how to protect his people. In doing so, he gave up his crown but not his griefs—he was still king of those!

KING RICHARD II BY SHAKESPEARE[1]

I'll give my jewels for a set of beads,
My gorgeous palace for a hermitage,
My gay apparel for an almsman's gown,
My figur'd goblets for a dish of wood,
My scepter for a palmer's walking staff,
My subjects for a pair of carved saints,
And my large kingdom for a little grave.

---

1. Shakespeare, *King Richard II*, act 3, scene 3.

12. Take some time to come before God and ask him to search your heart (see Psalm 139:23-24). If you are desiring something or someone, tell God honestly what you want and then wait for his response. You may want to write down what God is saying to you.

13. What does this excerpt from *King Richard II* tell you about his desires? Do you think his desires were pleasing to God? Explain. Do you think he was placing his hope in God? Why or why not?

What do you desire most? What is God speaking to you about the desires of your heart?

14. Describe a time when you placed your hope in something other than God. How did you feel? Did you come to a point when you fell facedown on the ground, confessed your sin to God, and received his hope? Explain.

EIGHT

CLOTHED IN SOUL STRENGTH

Taking Possession of the Land God Gives

JOSHUA 24; EPHESIANS 6:18

In the same way, the Spirit helps us in our weakness. We do not know what we ought to pray for, but the Spirit himself intercedes for us with groans that words cannot express. And he who searches our hearts knows the mind of the Spirit, because the Spirit intercedes for the saints in accordance with God's will.

—ROMANS 8:26-27

Now that you have caught a glimpse of how to put on the full armor of God and have studied the first seven chapters of Joshua, are you wondering if your soul is stronger? Or do you feel as if you're loaded down with so much armor that you cannot move? Are you secretly afraid that God is preparing you for an enormous battle ahead, and you're not sure you're ready? Well, do not be afraid, but be very strong and courageous because we're about to uncover the dynamic power that fuels our new spiritual wardrobe. It is the same power that led the Israelites to victory after victory thousands of years ago.

The book of Joshua is divided into two parts: the conquest of the land (chapters 1–12) and the settlement of the land, which includes the division of the tribes (chapters 13–24). The major campaigns (or battles) elevated God in an awesome, powerful, majestic display of his sovereignty. They took seven years from the time the Israelites entered the Promised Land. According to Joshua 11, Joshua "took the entire land…and he gave it as an inheritance to Israel according to their tribal divisions" (verse 23). The last line of Joshua 11 tells us, "Then the land had rest from war."

From that point on, the Israelites were to settle in the land God had given them. They had seen God's power rip apart the enemy, and now God wanted to fulfill his promise to them. "Go!" he told them. "Possess your possessions!" Here's where the Joshua story can help us better comprehend God's power and his invisible armor through prayer.

BREAKING GROUND

What do you "possess" spiritually? What, if anything, is keeping you from fully possessing all God has given you?

POSSESSING THE UNSEEN

Now here's the twist in the Joshua story: You would think that after fighting so many battles and conquering so many kings, the Israelites would have wanted to finish things off, that they would have wanted to completely fulfill God's commands to them so they could completely receive his promised blessings. But the Israelites did not possess their possessions. They did not embrace what was theirs to embrace. In Joshua 18:3, Joshua asked them, "How long will you wait before you begin to take possession of the land?" Even at the height of their strength, when they could have taken over the remaining pockets of land and defeated all who lived there, the Israelites decided that the enemy who remained wasn't all that bad. The enemy's culture was somewhat appealing, in fact. So when the Israelites had a chance to drive out the Canaanites, they "did not drive them out completely," but instead used them as slaves (Joshua 17:13). The Israelites wanted the best of both worlds. They did not take a stand.

Read Joshua 24.

FIRST LOOKS

1. In your own words, describe the conclusion of the Joshua story.

2. Before God spoke his promises to Abraham, what were Abraham and his people doing (verse 2)?

3. Based on verses 12 and 13, whose weapons conquered the land?

4. Briefly summarize Joshua's exhortation to the Israelites in verses 14 and 15, and describe his resolve.

5. What did the Israelites physically possess that God had handed over to them?

CHOOSING OUR POSSESSIONS

God calls us to take possession of his gifts today just as he called the Israelites to possess the land he had given them. With this in mind, let's look at the choices we make with our bodies, minds, and souls so that we can embrace the Spirit God gives us and win the spiritual battles that lie ahead.

Making a Choice

In the original Hebrew language, the words *serve* and *worship* were used interchangeably. They signified working as a slave under a king or ruler. Considering that the Israelites *were* serving the Lord at this time in history, it's interesting that Joshua continued to preach "serve the Lord." Not fully convinced they heard him the first time, Joshua got in their faces and said,

"Now listen. If serving God is not your preference, your desire—then decide now!" (Joshua 24:15, author's paraphrase). Did you notice that there wasn't a third option? There is no neutral territory in the spiritual realm—you either are serving the Lord God or you're not; you're either standing or falling.

In his book *The Pursuit of God*, A. W. Tozer writes, "Within the human heart things have taken over. Men have now by nature no peace within their hearts, for God is crowned there no longer, but there in the moral dusk *stubborn and aggressive usurpers fight among themselves for first place on the throne*"[1] (emphasis added). Remember that this fight is against the rulers, against the authorities, against the powers of this dark world. Internally, we are fighting evil, and this is precisely what it means to be in spiritual warfare. If Satan is clamoring for your worship or if your selfish desires are demanding to be filled, you are in the midst of spiritual battle, and you have choices to make. In other words, if you are living as a Christian, no matter what your calling is, you are fighting a battle. You must take a stand.

We are worshiping and serving the Enemy if we are not choosing and desiring Christ with our hearts, souls, and minds, if we are not choosing our possessions. Because the Israelites failed to completely conquer the land during Joshua's lifetime, the new generation was easily lured away to worship the Canaanite deities when the godly men and women of his generation died. Do you see the principle for us? Not one of the gifts of this life—material objects, professional or personal success, physical beauty, relationships, talents, nature—should be used as the armor that protects our hearts and minds. All of these things should maintain their place—their outward place—while the invisible Spirit of Christ rules in us with his unseen pieces of armor. Joshua 17:12-18 shows that the Israelites did not drive out the Canaanites completely. They wanted earthly peace more

---

1. A. W. Tozer, *The Pursuit of God* (Harrisburg, Pa.: Christian Publications, 1982), 22-3.

than they wanted God. Isn't that the same attitude they had cultivated on the other side of the Jordan? In the desert the Israelites demanded that their cravings be filled. This demanding spirit was still alive during the settlement of the land. The Israelites' desire for material possessions and comfort in the Promised Land steered them away from driving out the enemy. Thus, in satisfying their own desires, they failed to receive the even greater gift of land God chose for them.

What are you possessing from the "old land" and trying to live with in the "new land"? In my own life, I ask this question in light of my relationships. When I glorify a past season of good relationships with friends and family, my present company of people comes up short. Several years ago, when God moved me from the "old land" to the "new land," I began to see that he was asking me to grasp a new perspective on relationships. If I failed to do this, I would not possess fully what God had for me in this new land.

Our hearts and minds must be free from everything but Christ and the inheritance he has for us. In other words, we must empty ourselves so that we can be filled. This is the paradox of the Christian life. This is why war rages in our souls. The powers of darkness struggle against the Spirit of Christ for highest priority in our lives.

Our prayers and our worship must flow through our *whole* beings if we are to fight and win our spiritual battles. Our spirits, minds, and bodies are closely connected. The mind is the part of us that engages in thought and reflection; it is the midpoint between our flesh (human nature) and our spirit. The spirit communicates with God on a higher, more intuitive level. Both parts play a role in prayer and worship. When Joshua insisted that the Israelites choose for themselves whom they would serve and then state their choice as a community in a written covenant with God, he wanted them to make the connection between their minds, spirits, and bodies. He wanted them to choose with everything they had. He wanted them to take a stand.

The word *choose* means "to select, to desire, to prefer." Since our minds are the seat of our emotions—the way we think, the way we feel, our attitudes—they need to be behind our decisions to put on the armor of God. We cannot be preoccupied. As Joshua reminded the Israelites, God is a holy and jealous God (24:19). He asks us to choose him with everything we have, and he gives us strength and grace to make that choice.

The Mysterious Possession Revealed

When Christ ascended into heaven, he promised that he would send "what my Father has promised" so that we would be "clothed with power from on high" (Luke 24:49). And what the Father has sent us is the Holy Spirit. That's the Spirit Paul wrote about in Ephesians 6:18 when he said, "Pray in the Spirit on all occasions." The Holy Spirit is part of our inheritance, our possession that we need to possess! This doesn't mean he is an object to put above our fireplace. He is the gift of God that we need to take hold of with our hearts and minds.

Many saints—believers in Christ—have traveled before us. I particularly appreciate learning from the great writers who came before me because of the way God worked through their minds. Their honest spiritual struggles for truth make their writing powerful. But these writers also allowed the mystery of Christ to stay just that: a mystery. They don't try to answer all our questions; rather, they invite us into mystery so that we can observe the inspiration of the Spirit of God. In this way, the art and work of the great writers teach us what it looks like to wear the mysterious armor of God.

Through the written word, believers have offered us a lens through which to see truth. This truth has been passed down from one generation to the next, and it all started with the Word, Christ (see 1 John 1). So here you and I stand on the battle ground of the twenty-first century with millions of "soldiers" who marched before us. We would be wise to study their strategies for being strong in the Lord. How strong would we be if we read Madeleine L'Engle and Kathleen Norris who read Willa Cather who read Jonathan Edwards who read John Donne who read Shakespeare who read Homer? The Spirit in which these people studied Scripture is the same Spirit by which Paul wrote and in whose name he commanded us to pray! The Spirit who led Joshua and the Israelites to the Promised Land and led them to write down the story is the same Spirit who dwells in you and me today. The Spirit by whom the Israelites prayed is the same Spirit by whom you and I pray. How does this Spirit, who is invisible, help us put on the armor of God?

In the Old Testament God filled people with his Holy Spirit at specific times and places. He gave good gifts and commanded the Israelites to embrace those gifts. Just as God fought for the Israelites to have their own land, Christ overcame death so that we could have his Holy Spirit on a daily basis. *God has given us the gift of the Holy Spirit to possess.* Do we fully believe this truth? If we did, you and I would not walk in fear. We would not read our Bibles casually. We would not treat his Spirit gingerly or think of his power lightly. We would embrace him, possess him, wear him with the strength he gives us.

The Israelites tried to wield the power of God without doing what he commanded—they wanted to live in the land without fighting the battles. Sometimes we, too, want the power of God's Spirit to work in our lives without having to put on his armor and get ready to fight. The difference between the Old Testament believers and us is that we have Christ, the image of the invisible God, and his armor, his invisible grace. This is the mystery that God has revealed to the saints. It's profound to think that Christ is in you and me. Exalting Christ is our goal in life; it is the crowning purpose of all our battles. Every spiritual battle we fight comes down to the singular battle of proclaiming Christ as the supreme Lord, the King of our souls, every single moment of the day. Christ is forever in our souls, and the way to exalt him is to wear his armor—to speak and believe his truth, to offer and embrace peace, to do the next *right* thing, to have faith, to pray with the sword of the Spirit, and to hope only in his salvation.

Read Joshua 24:23-27 and Ephesians 6:18.

TAKING IT IN

6. Before the stone was erected, what did Joshua and the Israelites do to let God know they were serious about choosing him?

7. What was the purpose of the stone the Israelites erected? What does this act of using a stone remind you of? (*Hint:* Think about the Jordan crossing.)

8. Why would the stone be a "witness" against the Israelites (Joshua 24:27)?

9. According to Paul's words following the description of the armor, exactly how are we to pray? How can we possess God's power at those times when we are tempted to possess our own?

10. In what ways is the Holy Spirit a witness for us today (see also John 16:5-15)?

LIVING OUT A COVENANT

Recently our family made a "covenant" with two other families to meet together twice a month. We share a meal—usually pizza—and while the children play in the other room, we six adults huddle together and talk about the Sunday morning sermon. Then we start asking one another honest questions about our spiritual lives, our marriages, our children, our commitments, and our careers. Often one or two of us admit to struggling with the discipline of prayer. That's when we start praying aloud for one another. I think it takes all of thirty seconds to sense the Spirit of the living God right in the room with us! We get right to what all of us need the most—prayer in the Spirit. It's a treasure for us.

Making a covenant as it's described in Joshua 24:25 literally means "to cut away an agreement." Something has to die for the agreement to be sealed or considered valid. In the Old Testament the Israelites cut into rock when they wrote decrees and laws. In my own life I need to cut into my independence and pride to make a covenant. This means praying with others, being vulnerable with others, and joining others in community to cut into the Enemy's power as we acknowledge the covenant God has made with us.

In Ephesians 6:18, Paul twice repeated the command to pray. When you and I "pray in the Spirit on all occasions with all kinds of prayers...

for all the saints," we are destroying the power of darkness in our lives. We are taking possession of what God has given us; we are not standing by while enemies feed off our land. God does not ask us to pick up his Spirit and gingerly study him. God has given us the *power* of his Spirit—let's embrace this power with all we have and all we are!

If God has placed you in a Christian community, are you "possessing" or embracing those people as gifts from him? Do you genuinely feel they are precious to you? Are you embracing the Spirit and praying "in the Spirit on all occasions"? We will fight many battles both within and alongside our communities, but everything we need for the fight is found in the armor of God.

⚘ MAKING IT REAL

Often recited by communities of believers today, the Apostles' Creed reflects the theological formulations of the first-century church. Early Christians may have based the creed's structure on Jesus' command to baptize disciples in the name of the Father, the Son, and the Holy Spirit. Like the Lord's Prayer and the Ten Commandments, the Apostles' Creed has been recited orally for centuries, helping to pass on the faith of the church, to unify the body of believers, and to affirm our covenant with God as his people. The creed went through several transformations during early church history and reached its present form in about the eighth century. One way that we can take a stand and clothe ourselves in soul strength is to internalize a truth-filled creed, both individually and with others.

THE APOSTLES' CREED

I believe in God the Father Almighty, Maker of heaven and earth. And in Jesus Christ his only Son our Lord; who was conceived by the Holy Ghost, born of the Virgin Mary, suffered under Pontius Pilate, was crucified, dead, and buried; he descended into hell; the third day he rose again from the dead; he ascended into heaven, and sitteth on the right hand of God the Father Almighty; from thence he shall come to judge the quick and the dead. I believe in the Holy Ghost; the holy catholic Church; the communion of saints; the forgiveness of sins; the resurrection of the body; and the life everlasting. Amen.

11. As you read this creed, what are you taking possession of? Which part of the creed is hardest for you to believe—to take possession of? Be honest as you think about how your faith manifests itself in your daily life.

12. Now write your own covenant with God—your own agreement to personalize the commitment you are making to receive his strength. If you are doing this study in a group, share your covenant with other group members. When you share it with them, you will strengthen your commitment to God.

FINAL WORDS

Do you remember the definition of *stand?* It means "to take an upright position, to endure." It indicates a pause or delay. Can you visualize the three-point connection between being strong, putting on the armor, and taking our stand? Putting on the full armor of God and standing firm are parallel actions that work together.

I want to cheer you on as you continue your journey toward soul strength. God has so much more he wants to give you—more than you or I could ever ask or think. I am praying for you as you live out your written covenant to the Lover of your soul. Wherever your journey leads, remember that Christ is in you and that his armor is clothing you in soul strength.

LEADER'S NOTES

CHAPTER 1: PREPARING FOR BATTLE

Questions 1 and 2. When discussing literature in a small group context, it's helpful if different people comment on the various literary aspects. For example, one person could describe the setting, another could identify the main characters, and another could identify the antagonist. This keeps one person from having to remember all the details and enables the group to interact with the material as a whole while each individual shares his or her specific literary focus. This approach can add greater depth and clarity to the study.

CHAPTER 2: A FOREVER RELATIONSHIP

Question 9. Ask for volunteers when answering this question in a group setting. It may be too personal for everyone to share.

CHAPTER 3: TEARING OFF SELF-SUFFICIENCY

Taking It In. As suggested in chapter 1, it would be good to have different group members comment on the various literary elements in this section.

Making It Real. You might choose two of these questions to talk about with the members of your small group this week. If you'd like, continue with two questions a week throughout this study. If you are working through this study individually, you might choose one question a day or a week to meditate on.

CHAPTER 4: REVEALING WHAT IS

Question 4. Narratives aren't necessarily told in chronological order. That's what makes reading them so interesting. Reading stories should be pleasurable, but we cannot help but analyze them. Joshua 3 and 4 have such a variety of patterns of word choices, repetitions, and tenses from present to future back to past, that any pattern the reader sees is helpful. Encourage group members to use their own backgrounds in music, art, science, and technology to find patterns in these readings.

Question 8. The repetition in Joshua 3 and 4 creates a picture of movement. The image it first created for me was the aural (sound) image of a symphony. Others will see it differently. Commentators suggest that the Jewish people reenacted this scene as part of their celebrations.

CHAPTER 5: MOVING FORWARD

Question 4. It's interesting to note that this was the first Passover since the Israelites left the desert. In other words, it's only the second Passover ever celebrated! The Israelites celebrated the first Passover with Moses forty years earlier when they left Egypt.

CHAPTER 6: DANCING OUR WILLS TO THE RHYTHM OF GOD'S WORD

Question 1. Readers should look for at least three choices that Joshua made: He worshiped, he listened for God's instructions, and he followed those instructions.

Question 5. In the Old and New Testaments, the mouth is often compared to a sword. Harsh words and sharp tongues are compared to swords in

Psalms 57:4 and 64:3 and in Proverbs 12:18. In Isaiah 53:7, the Hebrew word for "sword" is translated "mouth," an entrance, the instrument of speech (Exodus 4:11; see also Isaiah 1:20, 49:2, Daniel 10:6). Encourage group members to find more passages that refer to *sword* or *mouth*.

CHAPTER 7: GUARDING AGAINST SELFISH DESIRES

Question 5. Anne Lamott writes in her book *Traveling Mercies* that her two most common prayers are "Help me, help me, help me!" and "Thank you, thank you, thank you!" Yes, we are saved eternally from hell if we accept Christ. But the Holy Spirit is alive now to help us if we just ask. That's a form of salvation.

Question 12. God is with us today and loves us. He is real. He is holy. He is the same God who counseled Joshua. With that in mind, you may want to do the following exercise either individually or as a group after you finish study 7. Ask God to show you if there is any sin in your life that is keeping you and your church community from experiencing his blessing.

Write out Joshua 7:12. Present yourself to God and ask him if you have stolen anything that belongs to him. (You may need to think back to commitments you have made with your money or your time in regard to your church.) Read Achan's response in 7:20. If you have stolen from God in some way, make Achan's confession your personal response: It's true, Lord. I've sinned against you. This is what I've done : _____ . When I saw _____ , I coveted and took them. Here they are. (If your group would prefer to pray this prayer corporately, replace "I" with "we" throughout the prayer. God may show an individual his or her sin, or he may lead the group to a specific corporate sin that needs to be confessed.)

Chapter 8: Clothed in Soul Strength

Making It Real. If you are in a group, I would encourage you to read through the creed silently, and then say it aloud together.

FOR FURTHER STUDY

If you enjoyed this Fisherman Resource, you might want to explore our full line of Fisherman Resources and Bible Studyguides. The following books offer time-tested Fisherman inductive Bible studies for individuals or groups.

FISHERMAN RESOURCES

The Art of Spiritual Listening: Responding to God's Voice Amid the Noise of Life by Alice Fryling

Balm in Gilead by Dudley Delffs

The Essential Bible Guide by Whitney T. Kuniholm

Questions from the God Who Needs No Answers: What Is He Really Asking of You? by Carolyn and Craig Williford

Reckless Faith: Living Passionately as Imperfect Christians by Jo Kadlecek

Soul Strength: Spiritual Courage for the Battles of Life by Pam Lau

FISHERMAN BIBLE STUDYGUIDES

Topical Studies

Angels by Vinita Hampton Wright

Becoming Women of Purpose by Ruth Haley Barton

Building Your House on the Lord: A Firm Foundation for Family Life (Revised Edition) by Steve and Dee Brestin

Discipleship: The Growing Christian's Lifestyle by James and Martha Reapsome

Doing Justice, Showing Mercy: Christian Action in Today's World by Vinita Hampton Wright

Encouraging Others: Biblical Models for Caring by Lin Johnson
The End Times: Discovering What the Bible Says by E. Michael Rusten
Examining the Claims of Jesus by Dee Brestin
Friendship: Portraits in God's Family Album by Steve and Dee Brestin
The Fruit of the Spirit: Growing in Christian Character by Stuart Briscoe
Great Doctrines of the Bible by Stephen Board
Great Passages of the Bible by Carol Plueddemann
Great Prayers of the Bible by Carol Plueddemann
Growing Through Life's Challenges by James and Martha Reapsome
Guidance & God's Will by Tom and Joan Stark
Heart Renewal: Finding Spiritual Refreshment by Ruth Goring
Higher Ground: Steps Toward Christian Maturity by Steve and Dee Brestin
Images of Redemption: God's Unfolding Plan Through the Bible by Ruth
     E. Van Reken
Integrity: Character from the Inside Out by Ted W. Engstrom and Robert
     C. Larson
Lifestyle Priorities by John White
Marriage: Learning from Couples in Scripture by R. Paul and Gail Stevens
Miracles by Robbie Castleman
One Body, One Spirit: Building Relationships in the Church by Dale and
     Sandy Larsen
The Parables of Jesus by Gladys Hunt
Parenting with Purpose and Grace by Alice Fryling
Prayer: Discovering What Scripture Says by Timothy Jones and Jill
     Zook-Jones
The Prophets: God's Truth Tellers by Vinita Hampton Wright
Proverbs and Parables: God's Wisdom for Living by Dee Brestin
Satisfying Work: Christian Living from Nine to Five by R. Paul Stevens
     and Gerry Schoberg
Senior Saints: Growing Older in God's Family by James and Martha
     Reapsome

The Sermon on the Mount: The God Who Understands Me by Gladys
    M. Hunt
Speaking Wisely: Exploring the Power of Words by Poppy Smith
Spiritual Disciplines: The Tasks of a Joyful Life by Larry Sibley
Spiritual Gifts by Karen Dockrey
Spiritual Hunger: Filling Your Deepest Longings by Jim and Carol
    Plueddemann
A Spiritual Legacy: Faith for the Next Generation by Chuck and Winnie
    Christensen
Spiritual Warfare by A. Scott Moreau
The Ten Commandments: God's Rules for Living by Stuart Briscoe
Ultimate Hope for Changing Times by Dale and Sandy Larsen
When Faith Is All You Have: A Study of Hebrews 11 by Ruth
    E. Van Reken
Where Your Treasure Is: What the Bible Says About Money by James and
    Martha Reapsome
Who Is God? by David P. Seemuth
Who Is Jesus? In His Own Words by Ruth E. Van Reken
Who Is the Holy Spirit? by Barbara H. Knuckles and Ruth E. Van Reken
Wisdom for Today's Woman: Insights from Esther by Poppy Smith
Witnesses to All the World: God's Heart for the Nations by Jim and Carol
    Plueddemann
Women at Midlife: Embracing the Challenges by Jeanie Miley
Worship: Discovering What Scripture Says by Larry Sibley

Bible Book Studies
Genesis: Walking with God by Margaret Fromer and Sharrel Keyes
Exodus: God Our Deliverer by Dale and Sandy Larsen
Ruth: Relationships That Bring Life by Ruth Haley Barton
Ezra and Nehemiah: A Time to Rebuild by James Reapsome
(For Esther, see Topical Studies, *Wisdom for Today's Woman*)

Job: Trusting Through Trials by Ron Klug
Psalms: A Guide to Prayer and Praise by Ron Klug
Proverbs: Wisdom That Works by Vinita Hampton Wright
Ecclesiastes: A Time for Everything by Stephen Board
Song of Songs: A Dialogue of Intimacy by James Reapsome
Jeremiah: The Man and His Message by James Reapsome
Jonah, Habakkuk, and Malachi: Living Responsibly by Margaret Fromer
    and Sharrel Keyes
Matthew: People of the Kingdom by Larry Sibley
Mark: God in Action by Chuck and Winnie Christensen
Luke: Following Jesus by Sharrel Keyes
John: The Living Word by Whitney Kuniholm
Acts 1–12: God Moves in the Early Church by Chuck and Winnie
    Christensen
Acts 13–28, see *Paul* under Character Studies
Romans: The Christian Story by James Reapsome
1 Corinthians: Problems and Solutions in a Growing Church by Charles
    and Ann Hummel
Strengthened to Serve: 2 Corinthians by Jim and Carol Plueddemann
Galatians, Titus, and Philemon: Freedom in Christ by Whitney Kuniholm
Ephesians: Living in God's Household by Robert Baylis
Philippians: God's Guide to Joy by Ron Klug
Colossians: Focus on Christ by Luci Shaw
Letters to the Thessalonians by Margaret Fromer and Sharrel Keyes
Letters to Timothy: Discipleship in Action by Margaret Fromer and
    Sharrel Keyes
Hebrews: Foundations for Faith by Gladys Hunt
James: Faith in Action by Chuck and Winnie Christensen
1 and 2 Peter, Jude: Called for a Purpose by Steve and Dee Brestin
1, 2, 3 John: How Should a Christian Live? by Dee Brestin
Revelation: The Lamb Who Is the Lion by Gladys Hunt

Bible Character Studies

Abraham: Model of Faith by James Reapsome

David: Man After God's Own Heart by Robbie Castleman

Elijah: Obedience in a Threatening World by Robbie Castleman

Great People of the Bible by Carol Plueddemann

King David: Trusting God for a Lifetime by Robbie Castleman

Men Like Us: Ordinary Men, Extraordinary God by Paul Heidebrecht
and Ted Scheuermann

Moses: Encountering God by Greg Asimakoupoulos

Paul: Thirteenth Apostle (Acts 13–28) by Chuck and Winnie Christensen

Women Like Us: Wisdom for Today's Issues by Ruth Haley Barton

Women Who Achieved for God by Winnie Christensen

Women Who Believed God by Winnie Christensen

ABOUT THE AUTHOR

PAM LAU has a B.S. in English and journalism from Liberty University and a master's degree in technical journalism from Colorado State University. A former English professor, Lau is currently a freelance writer and speaker. She and her husband, Brad, who is a college administrator, live in Oregon with their three daughters.

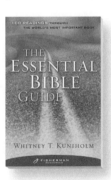
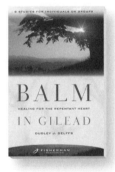
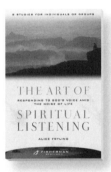

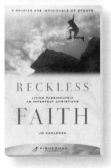